Who Are You?

Who Are You?

How To Get Rid Of Your Demons!

by **Wallen Yep**

toExcel
San Jose New York Lincoln Shanghai

RE Publishing
Carson City, Nevada

Who Are You?
How To Get Rid Of Your Demons!

All Rights Reserved. Copyright © 2000 by Wallen Yep

No part of this book may be reproduced or transmitted in any form or by any means, graphic, electronic, or mechanical, including photocopying, recording, taping, or by any information storage or retrieval system, without permission in writing from the publisher.

This edition published by toExcel Press,
an imprint of iUniverse.com, Inc.

For information address:
iUniverse.com, Inc.
5220 S 16th, Ste. 200
Lincoln, NE 68512
www.iuniverse.com

ISBN: 1-893534-02-2

LCCN: 99-62831

RE Publishing, An Independently Owned, Self-Publishing Company for writers of all levels seeking support in internet-related publishing as well as traditional modes and for aspiring Writers of the 21 st Century!

Why the title: "Who Are You?"

THE TITLE: "Who Are You?" is the command to an unclean spirit within a person to identify him/herself. Without knowing who the unclean spirits are, the person can be easily subjected to further entry and oppression by these unclean spirits.

There are many exorcists who cast unclean spirits out of a person, but there is a strong tendency for the unclean spirits to return. This is both scriptural and experiential. Empowered with the knowledge as to who the unclean spirits are, the previously "tormented person" can become the "tormentor" of these unclean spirits.

Who Are You? is a deterrent and a warning to the spiritual world.

Acknowledgments

My gratitude is extended to the very dear Brethren who stood by me, fought with me, and encouraged me to be strong and of good courage.

My appreciation is extended to Brother Bob Chew, a quiet warrior who gave of himself to the brethren and graciously prepared the publication of this book.

To our Beloved Deaconess Julia Chu, who demonstrated a great need for helping others and whose prayers made this book a reality.

To Yongsun, who brought me to the Lord and bore my weaknesses, I dedicate this book.

Preface

This book is going to rattle your sense of comfort and wake you up to a new world of reality—you have never been alone. You have no secrets to hide and you have been naked to a spirit world that has been watching and disrupting your life since birth.

There is no place to run and it is useless to stick your head in the sand. It is time for you to come out of your sheltered life and see what the totality of life consists of. This book will expand your perceptions and clarify the limits of your sensory world. Many of the mysteries of your life can be understood and the shadows of your fears can now be defined. It is time for you to take a stand.

There exists a spirit world that is greater in number than the physical world, the reason being the accumulation of spirits from the physical world to the spirit world. This spirit world is not constrained by laws governing physical properties. This world is divided by good and evil. God is real and has providential rule over both worlds and creation. This world, as we know it, is the primary dwelling place for the spirits that have been condemned by God.

Whether you believe in God or not, the truth in this book is going to give you a second afterthought. Physical life is finite, mankind has built a circumstantial world and has incorporated bridges of inference to encapsulate knowledge itself. Our sensory world is unable to perceive that which cannot be seen and touched, that which is incorporeal. We are defenseless against a very powerful evil spirit world that is hell bent for your destruction.

The scriptures are chosen as a parallel for two basic reasons: the statistical probability of the prophecies of the bible have proven to be an unequal truth when compared to other basic truths; and there exists no other literary work that has the descriptive or pervasive knowledge of spirits and the demons.

All of the activities of the demons are bad. They are worse than prisoners serving time for felonies. Demons seek to destroy your lives. There is little or no compassion or love, as we know it in the spirit world that supports an evil hierarchy. Hate, power, anger, lust, and greed are the order of the day. There is nothing in the physical world that is comparable.

The pattern is unraveling for this great destruction of mankind—they do not want anybody to ascend into the heavens to occupy the places of glory and honor that was once theirs.

Unless you are very spiritual and are able to: see spirits; cast them out; command them; and spiritually discern their presence and intent—you have no control over demons and other spirits. This book will provide you a shelter to protect yourself and place a sword in your hands that can destroy the demons. If you want to learn more about the world you live in, this may be your window of opportunity. They know the rules of the game, you may, unfortunately not know.

The unknown will be removed and in the process of removing this mystery—the demon becomes vulnerable. Yes, with the knowledge you are about to receive—you can defeat, cast out, or torment them as they have tormented you and your loved ones. It is time we take back our lives.

Contents

Acknowledgments vii
Preface ix
Introduction xiii
Chapter I. Contemporary Christianity 1
Chapter II. Doctrinal Overview 5
Chapter III. Pastoral Leadership 13
Chapter IV. Spiritual Battleground 17
Chapter V. Origin of an Unclean Spirit 21
Chapter VI. Methodologies of Spiritual Warfare 27
Chapter VII. Prayer 31
Chapter VIII. Laying On of Hands 39
Chapter IX. Commands 43
Chapter X. Participation of the Holy Spirit 49
Chapter XI. Satanic Hierarchy 53
 Warring Angels
 Man-Like Spirits
 Part Man/Animal Spirits
 Mystery Spirit / "Unclean Spirits"
 Frog-Like Spirits (creatures)
Chapter XII. Traits of the Unclean Spirits 69

xii   Who Are You?

Chapter XIII. Exorcism 77
        Prayer of Protection
        A. Authority of the Word
        B. Power of the Word
        C. Angels
        D. Scriptures for Exorcism
        E. The Commands
        F. The Subject's Behavior
        G. Response of the Demon
        H. Expulsion
        I. Building the Protection

Chapter XIV. Conclusion 103
Appendices 107
Index 109
Biblical References 113
One-Sided View of Christianity 115
Working Definitions 117
Other Books By Wallen Yep 123

Introduction

The anger of this world cannot be contained by the billions of poor souls who have lost their way. History has reflected this paradox lacking an attributable explanation. The inherent nature of man has been thoroughly inundated with: deception; destruction; evil; and false premise. Is this mankind's end and purpose?

With the enormous quantity of intellect available to provide answers and solutions, few prepositions have been found acceptable by mankind. We find ourselves constantly confronted with fallible ends. Science has been so limited by man's own intellect, that the assumptions previously held by evolutionists have proven to be seriously flawed. The net results of erroneous conclusions have left mankind to review coexistence with forces that are not seen, but that, by preponderance and historical reference, are undeniably present.

Archeological evidence can be seen to foment the science of knowledge to support the veracity of biblical truths. Patterns and observations provide a consensus of facts, giving mankind an insight into the spirit world as it exists. The data and learning precepts of this book can be a "lethal Pandora's Box" of power in the lives of those having the courage and tenacity to: understand; meditate; practice; and take a stand.

This book is not for "wimps", fearful persons, and the shallow minded. The source of knowledge comes from God, the Father. Unless this is fully understood, the power over spiritual forces can never be fully realized. The bible spells this out to all to receive the wisdom of truth, which has been the power to overcome all that exists in this world.

The master of destiny thesis whereby mankind chooses and commandeers his own destiny and life "lacks" the very powerful intrusion into these plans by spirit forces that are hell-bent on your total destruction. We have never been properly taught as to what and who this demon force has been. This teaching or knowledge is absent in the church, the place where everyone's spiritual growth is to begin.

An overview of the contemporary Christian world and incorporation of the experiential knowledge of the spirit world, establishes the background to bear the God-given power over spiritual forces. Without spiritual knowledge and God power, you have no power. There is no victory in helplessness, nor is it God's desire to see His children die from this lack of knowledge.

When we first become Christians, a process of sanctification commences and the people close to us begin to see changes in our nature and character. Our spiritual nature has been changed by the Holy Spirit. At the higher spiritual levels, there are a lot of spiritual gifts that can be recognized by someone else possessing the similar gifts. At some point, it becomes almost esoteric to understand, when someone of lesser gifts observes another possessing higher types of gifts. There are wide spiritual disparities amongst Christians.

The spiritual definitions of the Word in this book will elevate the scriptural understanding and spiritual knowledge of the reader. If you know the spiritual definition of the Word or the phrase in the bible, then the spiritual meaning can be extracted. Until this is understood, the biblical expositors may encourage all to take the safe way out by defining biblical terms and phrases by literal definition. This is not spiritual! A secular definition does not empower one with the Spirit of the Word.

Sadly, many ministers are not spiritual. The endless rationale of the Word to learn God's meaning from a God that is all spirit, without embracing His Spirit to empower the Word can only become a futile exercise of human wisdom. That is not good enough. If you have a church that continually teaches how the Word of God relates to our secular living, then your spirit is not able to grow. The purpose of your church after your salvation is to grow your spirit in the Word. If this is not being done for you, go to another church that can.

As our bodies grow, our spirit likewise needs spiritual food to grow. The spiritual food is the Word of God. With real spiritual understanding of the Word, the Holy Spirit filled Christian can be awesome in power! The content of this book will provide that growth for you. It is important for Christians to understand that Jesus was manifested to destroy the works of the devil (**1 John 3:8**). Wouldn't it make sense that if Christ moves you to destroy the works of the devil, then the purpose of Jesus is fulfilled? Is Jesus doing this now on this earth? How?

This book is written to provoke the reader's thoughts and understanding about spiritual matters. The reading is not necessarily easy and flowing, but the intent of the author is to raise introspection of one's knowledge about the spiritual world. Reading may be slow and sometimes rereading of sections may be necessary. Due to the very serious nature of the subject matter, the reader is advised to have complete understanding of the sections after Chapter V (5) "Origin and Definition of Unclean Spirits."

The reason for this style of writing is to correct the erroneous perception of the spirit world. A framework of Christianity and spirituality is provided in this book to enable a strong spiritual growth in your lives. The "Sword of the Spirit" is given; use it well.

—Wallen Yep

Chapter I
Contemporary Christianity and Doctrine

The Christian world has been sterilized from spirituality.

Spirituality is poorly taught in the seminaries. The churches are afraid to espouse spirituality, because either the ministers do not understand spirituality or have some other reason for not preaching it. The doctrines taught and preached are secular and involve considerable literal definitions. The net results are: we have become non-spiritual Christians depending upon someone else or awaiting Jesus to come back and redeliver us. The spiritual warfare against us is very great; yet, we are helpless and weaponless. We die, become disease-ridden, often hospitalized with some horrible sickness, and we cannot understand why God has forsaken us.

There are literally hundreds of denominations, each expounding its own interpretation of the Word of God. To this degree, the Statement of Faith was established to separate the "saints" from the "aints." The impact of each Statement of Faith has a very devastating effect upon Christianity, as it tends to separate Christians from other Christians. There is no single "good" Statement of Faith for any denomination. All have been divisive and argumentative. There is no inclusive Statement of Faith that is universal nor fully able to stand on its own two feet by itself. You must realize that all the rules and regulations are restrictive in nature—to limit the Word of God is not only wrong, but an act of ignorance. Someone wants you stupid; let it not be your church. Worship God and not your church.

Within the confines of a church, just waiting to explode out to the ends of the universe, are the multitudes of church fallacies? misunderstanding of doctrine, non-spiritual preaching, bingo games, barbecues, dances, and sewing circles. The denominations normally control both the doctrines taught and/or preached and the pastors. Then who controls the denominations? To exude efficiency and uniformity, the emergence of the administrators to control the church instead of the apostles or prophets, have taken the spirituality from the denominations and the churches. Both the denominations and churches became programmatic with a set of doctrines warning between a "conservative" to a liberal interpretation, depending upon which school or lack of schooling in theology is possessed by the administrators.

Can a minister be a good administrator? The way it is perceived by many—some make better administrators than ministers. To reflect upon this aberration of the denominations, just track the pastors who change their affiliations with denominations. Can a good Presbyterian make a good Baptist minister? Sometimes the changes are several times a year! Don't get me wrong. I know several of these ministers and they overlook the fallacies of the church, because they had just left one that was equally fallacious. They were there to preach the Word of God.

Over the past 15 years, there has been a substantial trend towards non-denominations. They call themselves, "bible thumping churches", but there is a strong trend by the laity and not the ministers towards non-denominations. The question to ask is why? There is a fluidity of doctrinal interpretation due to the continuing revelation of the Word. Until Jesus comes, this trend will continue. For those churches adopting a conservative stance and not incorporating revelations, clarifying eschatology, they must maintain rigidity on their Statement of Faith. The congregation is not sharing those executive policies made in a vacuum.

The case for people seeking a spirit-filled church to be closer with the Holy Spirit, Jesus, and the Father, is often countered by ministers who warn of apostasy and damnation for trying to be spiritual. The down side is that this exodus of the laity to seek spiritually filled ministers to become spiritual themselves, may fall prey to hoaxed ministers who claim to have the power of the Holy Spirit, but do not. I don't know which is worse—to be led to believe that I can become spiritual by misinterpretation or to stay with a minister who is not spiritual. My spirit tells me to grow spiritually and not to deny the power of God.

Today, most churches just preach what the minister wants to preach, as long as it can be done in 10–15 minutes. Few churches preach more than 30 minutes in the scriptures. Few ministers preach by inspiration of the Holy Spirit. The sermon is given—historical, secular or literal connotations. Some sermons are printed one month in advance. It is difficult to see how the congregation is "fed" with the Spirit of the Word. The emphasis to relate to the living knowledge of the congregation is far from delivering the spiritual meaning of the Word to grow their spirits.

It is agonizing to see ministers resort to screaming a sermon of salvation to a church that is already 80% plus saved! The personal traits of ministers—such as intellect, kindness, and patience—are a moving effect upon the hearts of many in the congregation. Regretfully, these attributes cannot be replaced for spiritual growth. Because of these attributes, I have seen ministers with the knowledge of the "Sword of the Spirit" not use this God-given authority/power to deliver the brethren, because of congregational perceptions. What do you think? Would you recommend to the readers to seek the spiritual church? I would.

In the 1990s, people seek the spirit filled churches, because many need real deliverance. Ministers can't fake a deliverance, but many try. It is very disheartening to be praying around church leaders that fake speaking in tongues. There are some TV evangelists faking the gifts of the Holy Spirit and laying empty hands on empty heads. Once I saw a TV evangelist knocked down by unclean spirits that he was trying to exorcise, he said he didn't know what was happening. I called and one of his ministers answered. I told the minister what it was and the minister hung up the phone on me!

Chapter II

Doctrinal Overview

In recent years, there has been a dramatic shift away from the "faith is everything" ministries. In perspective, there is a lot to be said for these Faith ministers. It is true that most people do not have enough faith, but what are the causes? I reflect back upon my Oakland home, which needed a serious paint job. Our deacon friend, generously, offered to paint the house. We were in the rainy season for our area, so there were frequent showers. As a result, the paint could not be brushed on.

Sixteen times it rained and our deacon called saying it was so rainy he couldn't come over to paint. "No", I replied, "just come over and the rain will stop and the walls will be dry when you get here." On each occasion, he doubted that the rain would stop, but he came over anyway. Each time the rain stopped and the walls were dry when he got to my home—16 times! No one knew after each call from the deacon, I stopped and prayed, wait, I didn't pray, but commanded the spirits controlling the rain to stop.

You can call it what you want, but it was not a prayer. I was exercising my understanding of the Word of God and how the spirit world works. Some might go so far as to say, I was standing on my faith, but that would be inaccurate. There are probably hundreds of varying degrees, to which one can exercise his or her faith. There is the gift of faith, whereby what is said from your mouth, the Lord honors it. There is power of the Word of God, but should one take the scriptures literally, historically, or allegorize the spiritual meaning of the Word?

By observation and from experience, unless you have knowledge of the Word, you cannot deal effectively with spirits. To begin, your position of authority, the power of the Word, an understanding of the spiritual world are all the prerequisites for having the power to fight. Having exorcised many spirits over the years, you have to "come off the blocks smoking."

There are many methodologies involved and many do work and many do not work. The basic reason for the multitude of methodologies is the enormous gap between spiritually understood scriptures and those that are understood literally. I have coined a phase that describes the type of healing described within this book—scriptural healing. There are similarities to general exorcism, but it involves the heavy application of the scriptures with a clear understanding of the spiritual meaning of the scriptures. With this knowledge, spirits become subject to you.

The "scriptural healing" method is the exact way that Jesus healed. Although Jesus laid hands, prayed, and enacted gifts of the Spirit—the most powerful method was "casting unclean spirits out" of people. This method, as described in **Mark 16**, demonstrated that Jesus wanted those who believed to follow in his example. It is "a sign" that will follow your belief. If you can embrace this short paragraph with your heart, the signs will follow you. It is an act of "casting out unclean spirits"—not an exorcism methodology but a sign of your belief in God.

What is the difference between exorcism and scriptural healing? It's the difference between faith and scriptural healing? Is it a gift or is it scriptural healing? The following chapters will provide a separation for you. If you cannot grasp this—it was Jesus teaching us the basis of healing—the method, the sign, the healing, the Word doing that which He wanted "all" those who believe to embrace His sign of belief. Do you know what I am saying to you? Jesus knew that most sickness was brought into a person by one or more unclean spirits!

Unclean spirits have emotions and very much succumb to their feelings. This one point convinces me that my definition of the unclean spirit is accurate. The exorcism or scriptural healing of unclean spirits is a serious matter. Spirits can attack you and enter your body and cause great havoc and sickness. I can only warn you, that exorcism should be conducted in the manner of scriptural healing, but also in the presence of an experienced exorcist. The more experienced the exorcist, the safer you will be.

The content of this book offers methodologies and doctrinal understanding for scriptural healing. The casting out of unclean spirits the exact same way Jesus cast out unclean spirits can be substituted for scriptural healing.

Doctrines are frameworks of truths from God and were never intended to be the underlying tenet for denominations. All Christians should attempt to understand the spiritual meaning behind "each" word in the bible. By this, the spiritual world can be understood and dealt with effectively, instead of the intentional avoidance of real spirituality in Christianity. If more people realize this, there would not be: such a great fear of death; so much sickness; so much violence in the world; suffering; misery; and yes, there would not be so many religions. Death has been the main perception of our entrance into the spirit world, if you believe this, then you should study the scriptures more.

As Christians grow in their spiritual walks with the Holy Spirit, the meanings of doctrines as you understand it will change before your eyes. The Word will become more intense. In most churches, there are no growth plans after your salvation for you to attain a certain or specific spiritual level. If you really want to commune with the Holy Spirit, your spiritual growth will sanctify you from other Christians. Do you know how it feels to be elevated so strongly in the Word that you realize you may feel alone?

Whatever doctrinal understanding you may have, constant communion with the Holy Sprit will teach you all things. The Word of God will feed your spirit. If you are fed by secular, literal, or historical applications of the Word of God—your spirit does not grow. Well some of you might say—what's the point of growing my spirit anyway? What good is it?

The sermons we hear in church range from: sex; crime; how to do good; how frail we all are; and the life of—where is our spiritual food? It is most intimidating to have a preacher yell and scream at you and then hold you at a certain spiritual level without growth. It is just as bad to have a very nice minister, coddle and sympathize with you and also keep you at a "no grow" spiritual level.

Spiritual discernment of the Word of God will induce spiritual growth. That means the minister should discern the Word of God for each sermon to "feed the flock." If the doctrine does not support this point, you cannot grow. This is not easy for the minister, because he never learned to discern it at the seminary. He and the denomination must direct his spiritual life and prayers towards the Holy Spirit to fill him.

One may get the discernment of the Word directly from the Holy Spirit or from another minister or laity who shares the spiritual meaning of the Word with you. True spiritual doctrine comes from God, Himself. One of the biggest flaws in the denominations, today, is the influence of the non-spiritual administrators, the capitulation of the Holy Spirit filled ministers, sterilized seminaries, and the lack of spiritual input from the apostles, prophets, teachers, and guidance of the Holy Spirit.

Mankind makes decisions, which they assume they are capable of supporting. What man has been able to support the spiritual interactions of the Holy Spirit? Can you control your own spirit, let alone the spirits of others? People must go to church to embrace the discernment of the Word.

In this way, their spirits will be fed and able to grow. It is a nice thing to have people respect you in a church, but aren't you fooling yourself? Watchman Yee once asked, "Who is greater, the person who has a great command of scripture or the person who communicates directly with God?" The person who communicates with God is greater.

Doctrine leads to communion and communion leads to revelation. The church today is seriously flawed with wide misinterpretation of doctrine and misapplication of the Word of God. There are great struggles in every denomination for the correct interpretation of theology. No denomination has been shown to be correct or inclusive. The very connotations of the "-ologies" create a premise base of study to the manner we establish science.

Science cannot explain a soul, spirit, miracle, healing, discernment, etc. and even in some doctorate theology colloquiums great efforts of scientific methodology are applied to demonstrate that God cannot exist. I agree, "science" has not been able to define God, nor prove what an unclean spirit is. I think it eludes the upper levels of knowledge of what mankind understands and perceives; however, God has revealed Himself to millions of people.

Within the church there is a battle to keep the mainstream Christians below the spiritual warfare level, which means "not to help you become spiritual." Some of the ministers taught by the author run their churches like a 9–5 job. By keeping the congregation together for a long time, that insures the retirement program of that minister. No one ever says, "I taught you all enough, now get out of the church and start your own ministries." Most bibles can be taught effectively in two years of weekly preaching and one-hour bible studies.

The spiritual portions do not require much time—maybe a few months at the most. The church should bring you to commune with the Holy Spirit, then the Holy Spirit will teach you everything thereafter. Just get them to walk in the Spirit and the Holy Spirit will commune with them. If the church cannot or does not get you salvation and then to commune with the Holy Spirit, then you better consider going to another church that does. What's at stake—your survival!

Doctrinal policies of denominations have failed the churches, the ministers, and the laity. The resultant response has created the formation of "consensus theology", to save the churches, the denomination, and to bridge the gap are the main concerns of the pastors. Are we supposed to follow the spiritual leading of the Holy Spirit upon the pastor?

The hope of you becoming spiritual has been replaced by a democratic process of other people. Folks, let me make it as plain as I can—all churches should be growing your spiritual level to enable you to fight the spiritual warfare that is raging all around you and your loved ones. It's called being fundamental, which matches physical sensory perceptions against that which is spirit. What do you think is going to happen under this scenario. Ever talk to a spiritual fundamentalist and ask them to lay hands on you?

There is a safety in the masses—if we are all wrong, it is not wrong! Then who can say they acted wrongly against the wishes of the masses? Is this what Christianity is all about? Keep in mind there were only eight people who came out of the flood. Don't become sheep and follow the errors of people.

Consensus theology draws its support from the congregation itself, whereby if it seems right with most members of the congregation it must be OK, otherwise

God would have told us. This type of theology unites the members into a singleness of doctrinal understanding—again, another possible tenet to establish the Statement of Faith. Numbers do not represent right nor truth. A position that Aaron's wife and the elders took against Moses as being the single spokesman to God. Consensus theology is a determinant of the "will of the congregation." Has anyone seen God providing revelation to the "will of the congregation?" It would be more appropriate to have the pastor fired than pervert or compromise the Word of God.

For years, a member of the church complained about the teaching on scriptural healing. His concern was the amount of time spent on demonology and spirits. One morning at 3 a.m., I got a call from him. He was scared that there was a frightful spirit looking at him. Although he was blind, he was instructed to command the spirit to somewhere else. After this, his criticisms disappeared.

There is no magic or mystery when one gets serious and studies the scriptures for their spiritual meanings. As you study the scriptures marked in bold in this book, you will begin to understand how Jesus healed the people. Doctrinally, most churches do not teach or preach scriptural healing; yet, **Mark 16** clearly tells all Christians first, **"that these signs shall follow those who believe", "in My Name they shall cast out spirits."** Where are the spirits to be cast out? They are in **you**!

How serious is this doctrinal exposition? It is most serious. In one of the scriptural healing workshops, it was brought out, that: we have a church system that condones and supports consensus theology; a denominational system that has sterilized the teaching of spirituality in the church; we have ministers untaught in spirituality and offering no spiritual growth plans for the congregation; and lastly we have developed the "one-sided view of Christianity."

Why is this so important? When you or your loved ones come under serious demonic attack, you have no weapons or means to defeat them. From this analogy, we have to get on our knees and pray until the sun shines through. Amidst all this praying, we have overlooked and ignored the fact that the Christians have already been given the power to defeat all the powers of the enemies, to be healed, by Jesus 2,000 years ago!

Being a frequent visitor at hospitals, there are all kinds of debilitating sicknesses and diseases afflicting Christians. With strong scriptural healing, these infirmities disappear "immediately" after the expulsion of the unclean spirits. Terminal cancer, kidney failure, itch, heart conditions, stomach cancer, anxiety, stress, and other infirmities have disappeared. There was a very gentle lady who was constantly sick. Once the unclean spirit was cast out of her, she was freed. She became very active catching up with all the things that have alluded her during her sickness.

Unless you have the "gift of healing" from the Holy Spirit, the next best is the scriptural healing method, which is available to all. This book intends to make you the "tormentor of spirits" and not the tormented. Know your spiritual discernment of the Word.

Chapter III
Pastoral Leadership

We simply would not be in this mess today had we received strong pastoral leadership. The pastor "must be Holy Spirit led" for the church to grow spiritually. Too many pastors capitulate spirituality under fear. This fear works against the church as a whole, the denominations, and the seminaries.

Where are the deliverance pastors today? There are more deliverers in the laity than those behind the pulpit. A sincere pastor would recognize who in the laity is moved and led by the Holy Spirit. Without pride, he should incorporate the full working of the Holy Spirit for the good of the congregation. If you see the pride of the pastor retarding the working of the Holy Spirit in the congregation, you should say something. One of my dear friends, Rev. Kenneth Dismukes, once shared a joke: "Do you know what is worse than the devil? A deacon, because you can cast the devil out, but the deacon keeps coming after you."

Having taught homiletic (courses) in the seminary, what exactly should pastors be preaching and setting goals for the church? Perhaps, after writing this section, it may evoke some comments from the clergy. Preaching is basically the pastoral tool for salvation—the most important thing in our lives. After salvation, feed the flock spiritually with the Word of God. Notice I did not say "faith development."

The greatest fallacy in faith is the implication to lean on Jesus to do the work and not yourself. Faith is for the creation of answers to prayers. Spiritual development is work. You need communion with the Holy Spirit, for He was sent to you to be your helper, teacher, and comforter. *I pray to the Father, I ask the Son, but I walk with the Holy Spirit. He is in you.*

Some years ago, someone did a very bad thing to me. To discredit my character, he said I talked to God. That was a nice compliment! Not only do I talk to God, but I also scream and cry out aloud to Him. Go ahead spill your heart out to Him, for He will hear a contrite heart. Presently, I still teach my congregation in an old hotel to follow suit. If your neighbors begin pounding on the walls to tell you to shut up, then you're OK! I used to go to the mountain to scream out to Jesus. Guess what? He heard me.

It has been said that one should step out of one's self and take a good long look at what you like and what you don't like. The concept is to know what to get rid of and what to keep. Look at the hearts of others. Can you forgive your enemies? I am still working on that one. It took a bunch of elderly and handicapped people to teach me how to show love towards a stranger. For that I will always be indebted.

Sometimes I feel and act like a saint and other times my circumstance arouse the anger and frustration within me. However, before I go to the pulpit, it is His time and not mine. I set myself aside and all of my circumstances. Whenever you step away from your circumstances, others see it with a mature understanding. One time I was going to confront a pastor's wife on some bad things happening in the church. My deacon, a very strong person said he was going with me. I said "No, because she is going to try and slap me." He said fiercely, "I'm not going to let that happen!" I said, "No, you must not be involved regardless what they do." What do we look like when we see ourselves? Can you serve all? Can you lead their growth?

Many in the laity have become deacons, deaconesses, elders, and even pastors. All members of the church have ministries—even the children. Children are the best investment we have. If you teach them while they are young they will be saints and evangelists for a lifetime. They become better persons. Their whole life becomes a ministry.

Just how far should you climb the spiritual ladder?—Climb as far as you can teach and help others. Watch over their souls and get their lives incorporated into the Body of Christ as early as they can. Grow their spiritual gifts for the edification of the church. In a real Holy Spirit church, all the gifts of the Holy Spirit are present. The size of the church does not matter. To be in a small church with all the gifts operating is a blessing.

The operations of the gifts of the Holy Spirit should be observed by all members of the church. Our church pianist used to ask me which hymns we should be singing for the upcoming Sunday service. I told her, "You choose it." She replied, "But I don't know what your sermon is going to be on." "Neither do I." I replied.

That was 20 years ago, and I never told her or her replacement which hymns to play; yet, each hymn selected was perfectly appropriate for each sermon. The sermon given was repeated by other pastors whether on TV or radio during the same week. In our church there are no leaders, except that of the Holy Spirit. It is He that leads, because our church allows Him to lead. Does your church allow the Holy Spirit to lead your church? Isn't that the way it should be? Don't let carnality rule in your church, only the Spirit of God.

With the interactions of the congregation, there are serious spiritual warfare and attacks. Unless the pastoral leadership incorporates spiritual weapons for its congregation, you will see a continuum of torment on the parish. The main inhibitor of a strong defense against sickness and diseases is the lack of spiritual knowledge of the Word. Christians fight the spiritual forces with anger and hate, no real power of the Word, no spiritual understanding, calling the enemies the wrong name, using the wrong weapons that have no effect—you will lose.

Chapter IV
Spiritual Battleground

There exists a spiritual world that is so powerful and awesome, that not to understand, teach, and preach it—is totally irresponsible. I speak to the hierarchies of the denomination, seminaries, churches, and ministerial elitists. They have all the wherewithal to study and address this most important issue—but they don't in fear of their own integrity.

You may wonder why this book seems caustic, I want to address the real issues without sticking my head in the sand. It is meant to break the barriers of benign contentment of those, who have all the answers but no power to exercise God's gift of power to deliver the oppressed.

For the benefit of the congregation, why doesn't the leadership teach and apply the healing powers of the Word of God; give the congregation spiritual weapons to get rid of the demons in their lives; grow the spirituality of everyone in the church; and allow the Holy Spirit to lead the congregation? Can someone stand up and answer these questions?

Put off the pride, the rationale, and being only hearers of the Word. Pick up the cross and the Sword of the Spirit and go into battle for the brethren. **Mark 16** states these signs shall follow those who believe, **"in My Name they shall cast out devils"**—exactly who was Jesus referring to? Ask your pastor when he delivers your spiritual food in a 10-minute sermon about some civil reform issue to placate your sense of security—yes brethren, God is still in control, but it doesn't mean your circumstances are going to allow you to survive.

For most of the good loving and strong Christians who have learned from workshops, direct biblical expositions on scriptural healing, and the spiritual world—the spiritual knowledge gained have elevated them to surpass years of ineffectual knowledge gained in the church. After you finish reading this book, you can view the world with your new incipient spirituality. My teachers, who were the best in the world, shared their deep in-sights/instruction with the author. It is my pleasure to convey the love they have for the brethren.

Most pastors cannot exorcise spiritual forces from people. They simply do not understand how to do it. They have never been taught. To my knowledge there are very few or no courses in the casting out of unclean spirits taught anywhere. The denominations which control the seminaries, remain stolid and demure when it comes to issues of spirituality. Yet, ask any instructor if he/she is spiritual and you will get a resounding "Yes."

When I first became a Christian, I told my friend that I just became a Christian and when I could pray for him. He said, "Oh sure." That night I prayed for him and he woke up in his penthouse with a bright light around him. Then he realized there was someone laying next to him and he jumped out of the bed. It was a figure of a man of light, who was snoring. He screamed, "It's God!" Then he started to rave, "Oh God, I will stop the sinning, the bar hopping. etc…" then the light figure disappeared in front of him and an icy cold shiver went throughout his body. The next night I got a frantic call from him about what had happened. Since this book is about casting out of spirits, I will share what had happened from another perspective in another book.

My same friend brought a professor of theology to my home to challenge the issues of demonology and spiritual warfare. I simply asked him, "Do you lay hands on the sick?" He answered, "No." I asked, "Why not?" It was not an issue to take lightly and he could not answer.

In Ephesians 6:12—for we wrestle not against flesh and blood, but against principalities, against powers, against rulers of darkness of this world, against spiritual wickedness in high places. It is not flesh that we fight against; it is all these things! What do you know about these things that are of spiritual origin? How do you fight a spirit? What has your church done to prepare you for this spiritual battle in your life? How does your pastor fight these spiritual battles? What weapons does he use? How many demons has he cast out, how many sick has he delivered? Shouldn't this be a priority in your church? What is the priority of your church?

When did the battle commence for you and your loved ones? Folks, it has begun for everyone, even those who are reading this book. Is your church strong against these evil spirits? Are these issues fully addressed in your church and by your pastor? Prayer is not enough! It is only a partial weapon, but not often strong enough to stop or even affect a demonic onslaught.

Do you think it is too outlandish to raise these issues? Look at the sickness/diseases in your church. There are other horrible events and activities, which enter your bodies and lives, which we cannot cover in this book. When I hear "We are blessed, we're blessed" by churches, I almost cry. How many brethren in your church are in the spiritual fight? Jesus started with 12, now there are about two billion Christians. Don't you care if an "unclean spirit" enters you and brings all kinds of filth into your life?

Spiritual warfare is a two-edged sword. You either stick with it or the spiritual forces will try to consume you and your loved ones.

The greatest hindrance to spiritual development is the absence of deductive or inductive logic available to the Christian. That which is spiritual must be interpreted into a framework of logical understanding and discernible knowledge for you. This book attempts to provide this framework for you. Without the revelation of the spiritual meaning of the Word, there is no framework upon which one can compile a spiritual meaning or understanding. Without the revelation of the spiritual definitions from the Holy Spirit, the structure cannot be understood or "seen."

Of all the professing ministers who claim to be spiritual, very few are. Most ministers have gifts of the Holy Spirit operating in their lives, but often there are laity that are gifted of the Holy Spirit. Before we [the author and his close friends] became ministers, many pastors would ask us many spiritual questions. In hindsight, these pastors were very humble and wise. Few had a comprehensive framework of the spirit world or of the satanic hierarchy. Even the great TV evangelists do not know what an unclean spirit is. Almost all who have made definitions about the unclean spirit were wrong. You can make your own judgment about this after you have read the book. The author attempts to provide the spiritual framework for you to understand and grow upon.

It is regrettable, but the author waited years for someone to write this book. Due to the great impact upon the lives of millions of people, I could not wait any longer. I could not stand by and watch the horror of demonic carnage against mankind. I hope that once you understand this book, you will pick up the Sword of the Spirit and enter the fight.

The most dangerous weapon that Satan has against mankind is indicated by Jesus in **Mark 16**, whereby Jesus states the believer's true sign is to be able to cast out devils from people. There is an evil spirit that is able to enter a person, influence that person's thought processes, bring sickness/disease, cause pain, can oppress the well being of a person until the person is so oppressed that oppression turns into possession, where a person gives up. This great evil is called an "unclean spirit." Where does it come from, what can it do to you, and how do we fight it?

Chapter V
Origin and Definition of an Unclean Spirit

Before you finish this chapter you may take a step back for serious reflection. If you grasped the concepts presented herein, you have elevated yourself into a spiritual plateau that all ministers must precipice.

Spirit is the intellect of man. When God breathed His Spirit into man, He formed a man with His Spirit. We are distinct from other creations and are equipped by the Creator with a power that transcends from the carnal world into the spiritual world. We have been endowed by the Lord with powers that are unperceived and undeveloped. It can influence the spirit world that is incorporeal to our sensory perceptions. The only problem is that we know so little about it, why?

Let's try to reason an answer to this question. Here's the situation: Imagine, for a moment that you were Satan. You were thrown out of heaven for trying to be God and then became the ruler of this world. No sooner had you realized that a proliferation of humans were going to take the very places in heaven that were once occupied by you (Satan) and your angelic followers and you retaliated with a plan to destroy the human race since God's creation. Here's the question: *With what and how would you destroy God's works?*

Would you have an upper hand if the enemy could not hit back at you? Is this why **Ephesians** states the struggle is not against flesh and blood but spiritual? If you can torment the enemy all day and all night long and he could not hear, see, feel or touch you, what are your chances of winning? Very good, better odds than snow melting at the equator!

The battleground selected is spiritual. The accesses to spiritual powers, weapons, knowledge, and a fully recognized method to fight have been destroyed in the churches themselves by professing Christians claiming to be spiritual but having no real knowledge or spiritual authority over the satanic hierarchy. Can any church claim victory over the satanic world?

Today, death is affixed to anything that is spirit related. These two meanings are not related and highly misunderstood by most people. Death is often viewed with physical aspects of the body. The body dies, yet, the spirit and the soul continues. They are not interchangeable. The spirit remains with man but 120 years. (**Gen 6:3**). People get scared about death and spirits because they have no power over them. Use God's given power and give the spirits the biggest fright of their existence! *Better yet, rid them from your lives.*

To understand what, where, and whom an unclean spirit is requires a framework of scripture and experiential knowledge. The reason for this absence of a framework is that it is non-inclusive but partially and critically defined by existing scriptures. One scripture that one needs to understand is **Gen 6:3—My Spirit will be with man but one hundred and twenty years**. This 120 years is crucial because it defines man's time on earth, before his/her soul goes to Sheol, the place in Hades for the unsaved souls to await judgment.

An "unclean spirit" is the spirit of a person who is not saved and has died. Since the spirit and the soul continue to exist, there is no warm live body for it to occupy. The "unclean spirit" seeks a body to enter and co-habit therein, often with the knowledge of the person whom it has entered.

In 2 Cor 5:8—we are confident, I say, and willing rather to be absent from the body, and to be present with the Lord. Paul states that Christians, once they are absent from their bodies, they go up to Paradise in heaven to be in the presence of the Lord.

The big question is: What happens to the souls and spirits of those who are not saved? What happens to those who did not have their souls and spirits cleansed by the blood of Jesus? The uncleansed (and unsaved) spirits became the unclean spirits in the bible when they died. By their rejection of Jesus as Lord, their spirits and souls were not atoned by the death of Jesus on the cross.

The answer is not in the King James Bible, but is clearly spelled out by the Catholic Bible, St. Jerome version, 4th edition containing the Apocrypha. **2 Esdras 7:79–87—let me explain first about people who had no use for the ways of the God Most High and hated those who worshipped Him. There is no place where their souls can go for rest; they must wander around forever in torment and grief and sorrow.**

Their torment will progress in seven stages: First, they ignored the Laws of God Most High; Second, they can no longer make a sincere repentance and obtain life; Third, they see the reward stored up for those who put their faith in the covenants of God Most High; Fourth, they think about the torment that has been stored up for them in the last days; Fifth, they see angels guarding the homes of other souls in complete silence; Sixth, they recognize that they must soon be tormented; Seventh, and worst of all, when they see the glory of God Most High, they are sick with remorse and shame. They cringe in fear because while they were living, they sinned against Him. And now they are about to come before Him to be judged on the last day.

The 120 years is very important, since it determines the life span of the souls and spirit of the person who has died. If an *unsaved person* dies at 40 years old, their spirit has 80 years remaining to wander the earth. At 120 years old, this unclean spirit must go down to Sheol to await judgment by Jesus. In many exorcisms, the unclean spirit tells how many years they have remaining before they go down to Sheol.

Unless this concept of "unclean spirits" is understood, just exactly how would you exorcise an unclean spirit? *Only an unclean spirit can incarnate into human beings.* Angelic beings cannot. The definition that an unclean spirit is a fallen angel or a spirit being not having died is false. There is no proof nor scripture that unclean spirits are fallen angels. The angelic spirits operate at a different level and forcibly direct the spirits of people that just died into people. Why? Why is an unclean spirit one of the most dangerous weapons of Satan?

I once read a book about the last days. Satan has developed a cyclotronic communication system that will enter and destroy mankind. Folks, Satan had this system after

Adam and Eve. It works better than any computerized system today—high tech, low tech or no tech—since a human spirit comes out of a person at death.

What is the purpose of the unclean spirit in living people? From the numerous accounts of exorcisms—there is a developing pattern—they want to kill, make people sick, destroy your lives, and take over the body they enter. The objective here is to possess their new victim's bodies. The world is full of persons acting like other persons, being totally out of character. Can you guess what is happening?

There are people who you could ask for their names and they give you a completely different name, why? Multiple personality syndromes, schizophrenics, Alzheimer's patients, and numerous unclassified types of mental disorders are some of the reasons/explanations. Can you guess what is happening? It has nothing to do with the mind. We read about people who have committed heinous crimes and they do not know why they acted in such an extreme way? Can you guess what is happening?

Most exorcisms have the same patterns. The unclean spirit wants to kill the person whom they have entered. People in great despair, cannot understand why things are so strange for them, that they seem to be "losing their minds." Anger, frustration, lack of control, depression, regression, and finally possession occurs. Do you know anyone who has often acted out of character and done things they have never done before?

The bible gives accounts of unclean spirits possessing people. They struggle so much that they go bonkers. What did Jesus do? He cast out the unclean spirits and the people were healed. He cast out the unclean spirit from the Maniac of Gedara and he became normal again. Without an in-depth understanding of the scriptural meaning of the Word of God, Christians who are not gifted may find it exceedingly difficult to exorcise an unclean spirit.

As did the seven sons of Sceva, the priest in the book of **Acts 19**, the unclean spirits will come out against you with all they have. I have seen great and famous pastors knocked down because they tried to exorcise an unclean spirit. Yes, the unclean spirit can enter you. In one exorcism, the unclean spirit defiantly spoke that he was an emissary from Satan. Can you understand how serious exorcism is?

The most apparent characteristic of unclean spirits is that they are the biggest liars you will ever meet. Do you know why psychics, spiritualists, and fortunetellers can never make a 100% prediction? The unclean spirits they are communicating with are lying to them! The spirits cannot stop lying. Why? They lie to Christians and non-Christians alike. All the spirits that the fortunetellers, spiritualists, and psychics are communicating with are all unclean spirits or spirits of persons condemned by God. They can never go to heaven. Torment and the Lake of Fire is awaiting them. All spirits that astro-flighters see and talk with are condemned spirits.

Keep in mind, the Christian spirits go directly up to heaven, while the unclean or unsaved spirits remain. The "transcended master spirits" are also condemned by God. Any spirit outside of heaven is condemned to judgment by God. There are no old timers. Why? The 120-year rule is in place. After 120 years, the unclean spirits go to Sheol.

What should you as a person of the 1990s conclude? In only one religion in the world, did the deity come back to life after he died. All those before and after, died and never had the power to return to life. Why? Jesus was God. How come, for the former religions, the deceased prophet or god could not communicate anymore with their followers? Again, the 120-year rule. If you had chosen a religion, compare all their attributes and would any be able to bring you into heaven? Don't waste your time or your life!

By scripture, there are several spiritual levels that exists. In each level, the objective and function are different, but still centered around a common goal—the propagation of the satanic character still continues—to lie, kill, steal, and destroy. Isn't that what is happening to the world today?

Isn't it a wonder, can there be any continuum of life with so much widespread hatred, anger, lying, stealing, pride, killing, selfishness, envy, evil, and lust? Are you not wise enough to understand at this point in your life—the end can only be total destruction? There is nothing to build for or upon under this scenario. It is time to wake up and know the real enemy.

Chapter VI
Methodologies of Spiritual Warfare

Warning: The various methodologies presented herein are *not to be used without the presence of an experienced exorcist, nor towards any Non-Christian.* Considerable scriptural understanding is required to conduct exorcisms, it must always be done with in-depth knowledge of the spiritual world. To venture outside of this warning can open your lives to entry by spirits. **The battle commences here.**

Until you have acquired the breadth of this book, your lives have been tormented. When the spirits asked Jesus in **Matthew 8:29—what have we to do with You, Son of the Most High, have You come to torment us before our time?** At that time only Jesus could "torment" the spirits, why? Because He had authority over the spirits as the Son of God. There were psychics, spiritualists, astro-flighters, diviners and fortune tellers in contact with spirits.

By scriptural inference, no one had authority over the spirits until Jesus came. Also this is the source of authority over spirits for us today. There are many other religions, both prior to the time of Jesus and today, who claim authority over spirits. This is false and deceptive. Only the authority of Jesus and the power of His Word have authority over spirits. For example, I met an African Minister, who had good knowledge of the Word and had an established exorcism clinic near Lagos, Nigeria. On Tuesdays and Thursdays, he would conduct exorcisms as part of his ministry. He has exorcised thousands of spirits from people.

One of my friends asked us to help some people, who were severely troubled by spirits. The Nigerian minister commenced to exorcise several of the spirits from a young man. After his exorcism, I asked him, "Have you exorcised all the spirits?" "Yes, they are all gone." I said to him, "No, there are still several spirits in the man" and proceeded to exorcise them from him. Sure enough, several more came out. What happened? The Nigerian minister really didn't know. His methodology was not scriptural.

Just what is scriptural healing? The exact same way Jesus healed the people, as described in the bible. This methodology is most powerful and very effective. You may note that Jesus commanded the spirits out and after they left the person—the person was healed! Do you know why?

In the Old Testament, the Israel nation was bitten by snakes in the wilderness. Moses was instructed by God to build a bronze image of the snake and declare that whosoever is bitten can look to the bronze snake and then would be healed.

When there was sickness in the desert, the people went to the priests. There were no pharmacies, doctors as we know them today. The healing was accomplished through the priests. Why? Because contrary to what is pronounced in church—sickness, diseases and infirmities are spiritually derived. One of the best scriptures for this point is **Luke 13:11–17,** whereby it was clearly stated that the woman had been oppressed by Satan for 16 years and Jesus free her. How did Jesus free her? Jesus freed her by removing the spirit oppressing her. This is healing in its most definitive form.

It is a great thing to be endowed with the gift of healing from the Holy Spirit. But what if you are not gifted? What do you do? Some bible scholars teach: you need faith to heal—this is very incorrect and wrong. For this very point many of the great ministers of today have expounded upon the faith ministries as the solve-all solution. It is not good doctrinal theology to presume this. Non-healing means you do not have enough faith. This is where many congregations and their pastors get grayish.

There is a plain and more simple way for you to heal yourself or someone else— use the power of the Word of God as Jesus gave us His power. The inherent weakness of the faith-is-everything ministries is the absence of spiritual scriptural knowledge. Most ministers do not teach enough or know enough about the gifts of the Holy Spirit and scriptural knowledge.

It is often said that there are doers and thinkers, but seldom both. If there was a real scholarly type who could devote serious qualitative study of the scriptures, he/she would not really understand the gifts of the Holy Spirit unless he/she was given the gifts by the Holy Spirit. There are many very powerful Holy Spirit gifted people in the world that cannot read or write. They have both the understanding and experience of the gifts of the Holy Spirit.

There are a rare few in the world that have obtained both high spiritual gifts and tremendous scriptural knowledge. This would be what I would call a "world class" minister. The few ministers whom I have met in this small category have read "only the bible" several hundred times. I am not discussing about collegial level research in the word, but simply the bible itself. With the contradictions that exists amongst scholars of theology, there is no one who has it together, none. One should read the bible constantly and realize it is the Holy Spirit that will teach you the spiritual meaning of the word.

If there was a choice to choose who is more spiritual, always choose the Holy Spirit filled person. Scholastic dissertations are greatly flawed by traditional scientific methods of inference and deductions. Neither of which can establish real spiritual knowledge. During one of my remaining classes for a masters in Christian study, my wife came to pick me up and also sat in, a student asked the professor, "Sir, what is heaven like?" The professor looked about the room and after one minute shrugged his shoulders and said, "I don't know." In one of the doctoral colloquium courses, established proof of the non-deity of Jesus Christ. Since I already had two masters, my time was better spent elsewhere.

Someone who can communicate with the Lord wins hands down every time, over the three-striped robed ministers. Upon your completion of this book, go have a spiritual talk with your minister. If he criticizes the content in this book, then ask him how he delivers those that are under Satan oppression and how many he has delivered in the church. The heavily concentrated ministers who lean upon psychology and behavioral science as a plausible explanation has little spiritual knowledge and no understanding. Those who have expository errors in their sermons, teachings and doctrinal knowledge and do not admit it are very dangerous. There are no know-it-alls—none exists.

Most Christians may not have read the bible or have a literal understanding of the scriptures. New founded Christians are greatly exposed to fundamental doctrinal errors and so-called statements of faith restrictions that contain the growth direction of their Christian depth. If you tell a new Christian not to go near the tongue-speaking types—it may be years before they develop their own biblical understanding that would include tongues. I hear so many fundamentalists that criticize tongues; yet, they themselves have never experienced the gift of tongues from the Holy Spirit.

There is a vehement radio preacher who condemns tongues, but never had the experience himself. Does he really know? There must be 20 persons per week who call him up and get into a radio argument with him. Had he experienced tongues, then it would be from experiential knowledge that he opposes tongues. Since his knowledge is not from experience but from his literary conclusions, does he really know? During my exposure as a new Christian, it was very difficult for me to know who was correct and who was wrong. Despite having read hundreds of Christian books during the first year after accepting Jesus, it is still difficult to know, except those that are spiritual.

The Holy Spirit has shown the powers of the gifts in my life. Since the topic of the book limits a discussion on these gifts, it is most powerful to combine the gifts of discernment, knowledge, and healing with this subject. If you want to become a powerful exorcist, you must petition the Father for these gifts. God has created mankind with spiritual powers that are inherent. Little is known about these powers, but people have accomplished amazing things through them.

For those who had spiritual knowledge prior to becoming a Christian, even non-Christians, man has shown an ability to transcend the corporeal world. Everyone has at some point experienced an ability to know what was going to happen prior to the event. Everyone has been able to reach out to someone else far removed from us and touch them. This may not be real Holy Spirit knowledge, especially prior to becoming a Christian. A very famous author once wrote that he does not want anyone to pray for him because of the unpredictability of this "spiritual force" within us. It is not understood nor do the King James versions have an inclusive answer for this. Just keep this in your mind that it exists and it is an inherent spiritual force of man.

Chapter VII
Prayer

There is nothing more powerful in this world than prayer and fasting. There is also nothing more misunderstood than prayer and fasting. For the Christian, if you had any gift to ask from God it would be prayer. It is impervious to the carnal and corporeal world. The forces external to us cannot stop this powerful force. It is God given and God directed. We don't need to go through anyone else in this world to commune with the Lord.

When the curtain in the Holy of Holies was rent, at the death of Jesus, the channels to the Father were opened by the blood of the Lord. When Jesus ascended to heaven to be with the Father, mankind's intercession with the Father commenced. Prayer evokes the promises given and the petition to the Father for praise and grace. Martin Luther King, Jr. often cited the need to pray to have victory for the day—a point of communication and a determinant of grace.

During my visit to the leper colony in Asia, it was not my intention to pray for the lepers but to have the lepers pray for me. These lepers know they have lost their bodies, but because of their very great pastor, they have developed to be one of the world's strongest prayer groups. Prayers are incessant and conducted in extreme fervency.

I know of no other place in the world that maintains such fervency. These lepers have disregarded their bodies and pray in the Spirit. The pastor deserves to be awarded the Nobel Peace Prize for his great work and dedications. He became a leper but asked God to let him preach. God healed him and sent a mighty angel to destroy the unclean spirits from the lepers. Two thirds of the original lepers returned home to live normal lives. The residues have become some of the greatest prayer warriors in the world.

Prayer can be conveyed as either praying in the Spirit (tongues) or in language. It appears that the more effective prayer is in the Spirit; yet, regular prayer can be very powerful. The Spiritual prayer comes from the inner person (the heart) and seems to be unencumbered with the world or circumstances. The regular prayer often evolves around circumstances in our lives. The best examples of prayer can be described by King David in the **Psalms**. Very powerful prayer can be described by Jesus' prayer in **John 17**. Jesus taught the disciples to do the Lord's prayer if you do not know how to pray. Yes, God knows our circumstances but requires that we pray to have. You have not because you ask not.

In **Gen. 28**, Jacob dreamed that the angels are bringing our prayers up to the Father and when the Father answers the prayer, the angels return with the authority to answer the prayer. Your angel brings your prayer before the Father. Daniel had his prayer answered by Gabriel, but Gabriel had to fight off the Prince of Persia with Michael to answer his prayer. Prayer has become the massive interactions of angels, the satanic kingdom and the Father. To be answered the Jacob's ladder must be scaled. Angels must go up and then come down with the answer. The spiritual world is the battleground. Do you have unanswered prayers? Why?

The prayer examples used in this book are aggressive and quite frankly *if you are to be a tormentor and not a tormented—you have got to come off the blocks smoking.* Although I have personally seen and participated in exorcisms that would be the equivalent of a polite slap in the face with a perfumed handkerchief. The demons or "unclean spirits" within the persons are screaming to kill you and the person they are possessing—then they make haste to exit the person.

During one of my bible studies, an elderly woman of eighty-six started to complain that her leg was cramping on her. "Sister Mabel, get your bible and hit the unclean spirit with it!" Mabel lifted her Bible very slowly and equally slowly tapped her leg with the bible in a softness that would make you sleepy. Immediately, she said the pain left her.

Having endured a youth involving about 100 fights in the streets of San Francisco and/or Oakland—the methods employed are aggressive. My justifications for such aggressive methods results from the many horrible unclean spirits in people and what they are doing to the brethren. I don't get mad when I see a young girl crippled by unclean spirits, deprived of a normal life, a family gasping for air and peace, and despair in their Christian walk—I get even!

There is a great fallacy of the types of prayers to seek deliverance. To explain this, the following examples are provided:

1. "Oh Lord, Help me. Get these awful sickness and diseases from my being. You are Lord of Lords and King of Kings. Help me, Amen."

2. "Heavenly Father, free me from all infirmities and sicknesses. Let it be Your will. Amen."

3. "Heavenly Father, Lord Jesus, bind all satanic forces against me and loosen all sickness from my body. Amen."

4. "You foul unclean spirit in my body—I break all your powers by the Name of Jesus and I command you loose from this body, never to return and to take all sickness with you. In the Name of Jesus I claim power over you!"

Academically speaking, which prayer was most effective? Why?

#4 has exorcised many unclean spirits from people than the other prayers. *#4 is not a prayer, it was a command.* I did not ask the Father or Jesus to do this task for me, I used the promise given by Jesus (both **John 14:14—*what you ask Me in My Name, I will do it and Luke 10:17-19—I give you power over all the enemies and nothing shall by any means hurt you.***

If God gave us the power over our enemies and promised what you ask Him in His Name He will do it—why do Christians keep asking Jesus and the Father to cast out unclean spirits? They got it from their pastors, their churches, the seminaries, and the Laity. How about from Jesus? Did Jesus give this power and authority to you? Yes, He did. Then why are you asking Jesus to do it? Ignorance and laziness can be a deadly combination. I have seen unclean spirits remain the tormentor and the Christian remain the tormented because of this point.

Effective prayer operates within the Word of God and also within a structured framework of creation, both secular and spiritual. It is greatly to the advantage of the Christian to master as much as possible about his/her authority and powers within creation. To be extraneous to this framework, I do not have any knowledge as to what is effective. Prayers are often ludicrous and an embarrassment to God. One person in our church prayed, "Father, give me 3 million dollars and I will serve you." Another, "Oh Lord, here we are again tonight and I want you to do this and that for me."

Prayers are not fireside chats with the Father. Yes, you talk to the Father, truly and with great reverence. For years, most of my prayer life was prostrated on the floor, with my head on the bible. My fasting prayers were screams of petitions to the Father. He answered many of the prayers and at one time considerable replacement of prayers were made to intercede for others. Frequent on-my-knee prayers were made for others. During one of my bible studies, a lady asked, "why do you pray so loud?" "But sister, I'm praying for you!" "Oh, thank you", she answered. We all struggle in this life; yet, despite the notion that some are better off than others—don't you believe it. Everyone has serious problems and can utilize the help.

We all need the Lord to answer our prayers. But how does prayer work? In **Gen 28:12,** Jacob dreamed a ladder going up to heaven with angels going up and down this ladder. At the top of the ladder was God. When prayers leave your mouth, your angel brings this prayer to God. God then send angels down to answer the prayer.

A very important point is that God is the Creator. He creates the answer to your prayer and He sends angels to answer them as He did with Daniel. The spiritual forces of Satan battle these angels constantly and often prayers are delayed and unanswered. For this reason, you must pray incessantly until the answer comes to you. This is a battleground by itself. There are other battlegrounds, where spiritual forces meet. As you absorb the contents of this book, the spiritual battlegrounds and participants will be revealed to you.

Ever wonder about certain people that seem to mess up despite whatever they try to do or not do? They frequently end up falling into evil and mostly to the detriment of themselves and those around them. Our guardian angels assigned to us are fallible. If your angel sins, then your guardian angel becomes a fallen angel. **Hebrew 1:14** cites **"are they not all ministering spirits sent out in God's service, for the sake of**

Prayer 35

those destined to receive salvation?" These are your guardian angels. The sooner you realize their roles and responsibilities the better and safer your life will become.

Can you imagine the horror of having a guardian angel become a fallen angel? The bible has proven to us that angels can fall from grace. In an event, like this, such fallen angels must be removed or surrounded by other holy angels. The request in prayer for Holy Angels to surround us as a hedge, like in **Job 1:10**, can strengthen your life and protect your loved ones and property.

When I pray in silence, without uttering my mouth, my prayers are still answered. In **1 Samuel 1**—Hannah was crying her prayers to the Lord without utterance and God answered her prayer. An important point is that spirits can hear your thoughts as well as speak as though you were thinking. This makes unclean spirits very dangerous. Realize that both silent prayers and thoughts can be heard by God and also by spirits. This has been proven time after time by Christians.

People's thoughts can be deceiving. An unclean spirit enters and commences to suggest, interfere, change, and coerce one's thoughts. Do you know why people who commit heinous crimes say, "I don't know why I thought that or did that?" Because it really wasn't them! Know yourself and your own personality. Whenever you are "pushed" or "pulled" some unclean spirit is trying to change you. Prayer is frequently interrupted, especially prior to bible study, singing of hymnals, and for some very significant reason—before a baptism.

The purpose of prayer is the communion with the Father. Jesus opened the path direct to the Father and Christians can have their prayers ascend to His presence. One of the main reasons for "praying all the time" is the spiritual battle that is encountered by the angels bringing the prayer to the Father and returning to answer your prayer. In Pastor Howard Pittman's book, "**Demons**"—there exists a multi-tier level of a satanic hierarchy at five different spiritual levels. Angelic battles are occurring as you read this book.

In **Daniel**, Gabriel remarked that he was being buffeted by the Prince of Persia and he needed Michael to come to help him get through to answer Daniel's prayer. If they can stop Gabriel and require Michael to come in the battle, our angels may be having a very difficult time. Since Daniel's prayer was delayed for weeks, it may be presumed that some of our angels don't make it back to answer our prayers. Then pray again and again—until the answer comes. Pray for the angelic beings around us. Place flaming swords in their hands. Surround them with Holy angels in massive scales. Surround your loved ones with hundreds of Holy angels in great hedges as **Job 1:10—so that even Satan cannot touch us**. Jesus was not kidding around when He said, He could ask for legions of angels and they would come.

The angelic spirits around us are an integral part of the prayer. They bring up the prayer and they return with the answer, assuming they can make it back.

Angels are a very important element of our spiritual life. You must understand the spiritual world and begin your "working" with angels. Without this, it is difficult to believe you can call yourself spiritual. If you are the heir to salvation, you have guardian angels **(Heb. 1:14)**. The gift of spiritual discernment will allow you to see spirits; pray for it.

The other powerful spiritual element in your life is fasting. Combined with prayer there is no doubt you will become spiritual. Fasting removes you from this world and the ties that bind you to this world and your body. The spirit and soul must be elevated closer to God. The results of fasting allow spiritual gifts to come upon you in tremendous force. The best time to grow your gifts is fasting and praying. At this point your own spiritual being and soul becomes very powerful. When you have serious difficulties, praying and fasting will help you overcome such difficulties. Many of the spiritual gifts can help you overcome circumstances. I recommend the readers to power up and then deal with the major issues of your life.

Fasting has been with us since Adam and Eve. Many of the great patriarchs, ministers, and laity have been the recipients of God's grace by fasting. In the Apocryphal books, angelic messengers from God would tell the prophets to fast before they receive an answer from God or to be in the presence of the angel.

The definition for fasting has been expanded in **Isaiah 58**. The fasting is to "afflict your soul", but, God prefers "you" to help those in deep affliction and should you hear the call, you will be raised up and exalted. As a beneficiary of **Isaiah 58**, God keeps His Word.

Depart from the "if it is Your will, Lord" prayers. **God gave us power over all the power of the enemies and nothing shall by any means hurt you—Luke 10:17-18.** Why haven't you learned how to use this power? Because some minister said it was only given to the seventy disciples? In **Mark 16:16-17** stipulates that—**these signs shall follow those who believe, in My name they shall cast out demons**. Do they cast out demons in your church? Why not? After reading this book, you will clearly know who are the unclean spirits and how they are bound in a spiritual world, upheld by His Word.

The best time to pray is in the morning before the sun comes up. Many answered prayers have been in the early mornings about 5 a.m. Jesus prayed in the early hours also. It is mentioned several times in the bible about early morning prayer. Martin Luther King, Jr. in his writings mentioned that he had to pray for two hours in the morning each day or Satan would get the better of him during the day. Having been taught by Korean ministers in Southern Baptist churches, I learned to shout out my prayers, especially in the mountains and at home.

When you enter spiritual battle for yourself it's tough, but when you enter spiritual battle for someone in dire straits, the problems and opposition become mountains. Prayer helps you strengthen your fight. Is it your spirit that you strengthen, your soul, or your body? All of these. Your house, your pets, your loved ones, your friends, members of your church and your neighbor.

Pray for the President whether or not you voted for him or like him. He is the guy with his finger on the button. Pray for the enemies, its like putting heaping coals on their head. Prayer must have purpose. Prayer is for the tangible and intangible in this life. Never pray against anyone or their angel will testify to the Father for them. You would be wrong and they will be right before the Father, God Almighty, The Creator.

Take the time out to be sure that you have been praying correctly. King David's prayers in the Psalms are good teachers for us. They are strong prayers and he moved the Father's heart. Elijah's prayers can teach us about how to pray—totally submitted. Your prayers should be submitted to God, by this I mean submitting your heart to God, reverencing Him, and praise Him for His grace. Paul teaches us to submit ourselves to God and then "resist the devil" and he will flee. The prayers of the Bible teaches us how to pray for the nation, our lives, our circumstances, other Christians and our enemies.

Praise is to be a constant element of your prayer for it to bring the blessing of God into our lives. Petitions are necessary to deal with circumstances beyond our reach. As you read the end of **Mark 16—and Jesus working with them confirming His word with signs and wonders.** Have the Lord confirm His Word in your life, also with signs and wonders. Offer up sacrifices of thanksgiving for His grace. Forgiveness, praise, petition, and thanksgiving create a comprehensive prayer to build upon.

Chapter VIII
Laying on of Hands

Many churches and ministers do not lay hands on the members of the congregation. The basic purpose of laying of hands has been: the imparting of the Holy Spirit; remission of sins; and the healing of sickness. This section will cover a narrative on this.

In the sacrifices offered to God, the priest would lay his hands on the head of the animal to be offered. The actual laying of hands was to impart the sins of the people to the animal to be sacrificed. In the Old Testament, the laying of hands was linked to the remission of sins through a substitute (an animal).

New Testament remission of sins is accomplished by water baptism. The New Testament laying of hands induced the imparting of the Holy Spirit. Paul in Acts imparted the Holy Spirit to water baptized Christians, who had no knowledge of the Holy Spirit.

When ministers are ordained, other ministers lay hands upon their heads for imparting of the Holy Spirit and for blessings. The laying of hands on the heads of our children, like Joseph, was an imparting of the blessing. Once given, it could not be taken back.

The scriptures carry caution in the laying of hands on people's head, that they should not bear the sins of those whom their hands touch.

The central theme of this book is the laying of hands for healing. The laying of hands on people for healing does not carry the same meaning. It is a spiritual act. When I lay hands on people, my hands turn into a golden fire. During scriptural healing, the unclean spirits are very fearful of my hands touching them. They begin to hyperventilate at an extreme and shake all over. When I lay hands on their heads, normally the unclean spirit departs immediately. In some occasions they do not depart, until I touch the forehead.

Many gifted ministers lay hands on people to impart the Holy Spirit. During a tour of churches, "everyone" from children to long time elders spoke in tongues. There were about 400 persons speaking in tongues during that service. When the Holy Spirit imparts to someone else, you could feel it (almost an electric-type current) leave your arms and hands. During a strong prayer for our deacon in the hospital, a ball of fire came out of my wife's hands into the cancer area of his body. He was healed and left the hospital after the doctors declared he had only hours to live.

The laying of hands by some ministers after exorcism to impart the Holy Spirit is being practiced. Why? After casting out the unclean spirit, the ministers want the person to be filled with the Holy Spirit. Although, it is not a main theme of this book, tongue speech with the intercession of the Holy Spirit is a very powerful deterrent to unclean spirits. Would you re-enter a person after you see the Holy Spirit of God working in them?

There are 16 types of tongue speech. The interpretation of tongues is probably the rarest of gifts of the Holy Spirit. I have seen it only in the most gifted of persons. Most Christians who have this gift have spent tremendous amounts of time fasting and praying.

During my trip to Asia in 1982, by the laying of hands on people's heads, more than 700 persons spoke in tongues. I was once asked to go to a hospital to pray for the sick. At my mentor pastor's request he asked that I lay hands on an older gentleman. As soon as I touched him, I felt no spirit of the Holy Spirit in him, so I immediately took my hands off him and just prayed for him. After going outside, the pastor asked me, "What happened?" I replied, "He had no Spirit, he's not a Christian!" The pastor answered me and said he was a Buddhist. "Pastor, what's the matter with you, I can't lay hands on him!"

Do not lay hands on a non-Christian it is very dangerous. Per the bible's New Testament, we are cautioned not to bear the sins of people by laying of hands on their head. My interpretation means non-Christians. The Holy Spirit is not a shotgun! He is our teacher and comforter. We should never just be laying the impartation of the Holy Spirit on everyone and anyone. Think about it!

If you have the gift of healing, then the laying of hands is very effective. As your spiritual growth becomes stronger, you will be able to just sit in a chair or be standing anywhere and the presence of the Holy Spirit comes upon you. In another book, I would be happy to describe the communion of the Holy Spirit upon your life and how to share some of the experiences.

A dear pastor friend has such a presence of the Holy Spirit, that he has turned to me on several occasions and answered my thoughts! If he sits in a crowded bus, he is sitting alone. No one wants to be near him. The spirits inside of people are fearful of him. They know who he is. Some members of his church have gone up to him and have passed out! He has laid hands on the sick and more than 500,000 people have been healed. I have seen him knock out 300 persons in our church in 15 minutes! He has laid hands on more than 12 persons and they came back to life! Is laying of hands powerful? Yes, it always was.

The gift of healing, the imparting of the Holy Spirit describes the contemporary usage of laying of hands. They are not the same. Some people can impart the Holy Spirit without the gift of healing. Your walk with the Holy Spirit is essential to impart the Holy Spirit. The imparting of the gifts of the Holy Spirit is as it (Holy Spirit) wills. You must understand this—the Holy Spirit works in you but not under your control. The more you decrease the more He increases. If you don't get this point, I seriously doubt the Holy Spirit impartation and gift will work through you. There are many ministers who place "their faith" on laying of hands and many are not healed. Why? You have to allow the Holy Spirit to work as He will through you and what you do.

In every Holy Spirit church, all the gifts operate in its members, regardless of the size. The laying of hands in your church should be an important part of your church to impart the Holy Spirit for healing and blessing. Whatever else you do, do not be disrespectful to the Holy Spirit. He is God.

Chapter IX
Commands

My wife was once accosted by another pastor's wife, who said, "In the Name of Jesus I command you to clean the kitchen!" She didn't know what to do but respectfully did whatever this pastor's wife asked of her. Sometimes we don't know whether we should or shouldn't do things. If you were a good spirited Christian, what would have you done? The pastor's wife was wrong to do this, but she anyway accomplished her purpose. Let us not abuse and berate the Holy Name of the Lord, but bow in reverence.

As tough as some people call me, I would not have the guts to do this nor the irreverence. When I was young, it was an easy thing for me to jump into a fight. After a while, the mechanics of fighting became easy and as I matured it became very wrong to hurt someone for an act of stupidity or rudeness. After the years of college, the pen became a stronger instrument of power than the physical force. The words of men became the focus of strength in my life and it replaced my previous understanding of power.

It was a good thing to teach those who understood less, the perspectives of my life as it matured my understanding of all things. In my teens, my perspective centered around the circumstances that would bring into focus my growing identity. In my twenties, the competitive levels around me would mold my next 15 years (intermediate goals). In my thirties, achievements were important symbols of my life. In my forties, failed dreams and aspirations brought my understanding to realistic expectations and personal limitations. My next phase of maturation will allow my role in society to be able to provide effective restructuring of priorities that I can contribute towards. With this in mind, you may understand the background of that which has proved effective in my spiritual walk.

It was about 12 years ago, that my friend asked us to help his family. He had a brother who graduated in mathematics from UC Berkeley but became involved in drugs and had taken "angel dust" PCB. At best he was incoherent. He would get up every two to three hours and do pushups. Spirits would appear everywhere. He would do very kinky things at all hours and required constant supervision. We prayed, laid hands, sang hymns, rebuked the spirits and everything that we could possibly do to try and bring him back. Many evangelists would come and pray over him. After a few months, he became more sedate with many of his previous habits broken.

He went back home and was later found dead. This young man moved my heart so much, that I said to my associate, "Harold, if God would give me the power to heal people like him, I would quit and become a dedicated minister."

Nothing happened for two years, but an enormous amount of teaching was introduced to my life. My mentor pastor came to my home one day and sat on the steps in front of my house. "What are you doing there, Pastor?" He said, "God told him to leave his church of 5,000 and to come to teach me the bible. If I kick him out, he would come back and wait until I was ready to learn the bible." He stayed with us for two years, to teach only my wife and I the bible, day and night. World-class pastor and evangelists would come to our humble home and pray for us and teach us.

One night I went to a small church of 300 to see a dear pastor/friend conduct a revival. In 15 minutes he exorcised the spirits out of everyone. He would "command" the unclean spirits to speak out of the mouths of the people. My eyes almost came out of my sockets at the unclean spirits speaking out of the mouths of people who I knew very well. That night the lame could walk and the deaf could hear. This was not chicanery or fake. I knew these people and some of the most desperate things were being said by the unclean spirits, before they were cast out. After the unclean spirits left the people, the people were healed. Their sicknesses also left them. This was exactly the same way Jesus healed in the scriptures.

Matthew 10:1—and when He had called unto Him the twelve disciples, He gave them power against unclean spirits, to cast them out, and to heal all manner of sickness and all manner of disease. Jesus gave power to the twelve—against, to cast them out, and heal. Unclean spirits are associated with sickness and diseases. Once you cast out the unclean spirits, the sickness and diseases leave also. Why? The sickness and diseases were brought into a person by the unclean spirits. **Matt. 8:16—when the even was come, they brought many that were possessed with devils; and He cast out the spirits with His word, and healed all that were sick:** Jesus used His word and cast out the unclean spirits and the people were healed. Today few churches do this, why?

In some of my workshops on exorcism or scriptural healing, it has been asked, "my faith isn't enough to cast out spirits." It has nothing to do with your faith. **Hebrew 11:1** defines faith, now what does that have to do with exorcism or scriptural healing? The faith-is-everything ministries are wrong. They have doctrinalized and categorized faith into a comprehensive doctrine or denomination is more like it. As the disciples were casting out unclean spirits, there were others copying them and they also were casting out unclean spirits—this means people who have "zero faith" can heal others.

That isn't what faith is all about. Faith is extremely broad based and is much greater than what these ministries make it to be—concise and self-contained. It isn't. You can "command" an unclean spirit to leave someone. It is scriptural and doesn't really require 1/100th of a mustard seed's faith size to do it. If you can tell your loved ones to "take out the garbage", you can command "unclean spirits" out.

Anyone can become filled with the Holy Spirit. Once you are filled, you have the power to cast out the spirits. There are no secrets. Yes, even your minister can learn to do this. The scriptures tell us how to do it. All we need is to have the fellowship of the Holy Spirit. Learn the processes and the context of this book well and you will become spiritually strong. Yield to the Holy Spirit and He will teach you all things. The Holy Spirit opens up your spiritual eyes and your senses to become a strong member of the body of Christ.

Should I pray, ask Jesus to do it for me, grow more faith or ask for God's will? Do none of these—just command! Jesus gave us the power in **Luke 10:19—Behold, I give unto you power to tread on serpents and scorpions, and over all the power of the enemy: and nothing shall by any means hurt you. Notwithstanding in this rejoice not, that the spirits are subject unto you...**

We have been given the power to do this, why should we ask anyone else to pray or cast out or command for us? If Jesus gave us to the power to do it, why are we asking Jesus to do it? Because some ministers, who don't know, told us the healing gifts stopped at the demise of the 12 apostles. Nothing could be further from the truth! It is contrary to the purpose of giving power and authority. The power and authority is given to you, you do it. As much as 98% of the church does not take up this power as it was intended. They have been led to believe that "once this lousy world is over, then I will be able to live as the Lord meant it to be." This is why Satan has victory over you. This is why the hospitals are full of Christians. After you have salvation, does the Lord want you to lay back and await His coming? The harvest is full but the workers few. If you really love the brethren (a stranger) and they are in need, then help them.

After you become spiritual and are able to yield to the Holy Spirit, the gifts of the Spirit will be working in you. You will be able to see spirits, know things before they happen, can discern even sickness in people, and know who is good or bad. Why should God allow His Spirit to teach you all things and know all things?

So you can flex God's power in you? That's not going to happen. When these gifts come upon you and you can see the unclean spirits causing sickness and disease in your loved ones—you get mad. It gives you the right motivation to "come off the blocks smoking."

In most of my scraps when I was young, it mostly ended with one punch. That is the way you should deal with unclean spirits, regardless who they are. When you begin to command unclean spirits—they will teach you how strong you have to be with them. Many world-class exorcists when they began commanding spirits will tell you, they stood there all day and night and finally the unclean spirit answered their command. Why is this so? As in thee **Acts 19:15—and the evil spirit answered and said, 'Jesus I know, and Paul I know; but who are ye?'**

For those who will read and understand this book, without being a Christian, it would be highly probable that this will happen to you. The evil spirit came out of the man and beat up the seven sons of Sceva. If you don't believe in Jesus as God, don't use any of the contents of this book for any such purposes, because the entry by spirits can destroy you and those around you.

The "command" should always be strong and inclusive. Remember: Do not traffick with unclean spirits, the Lord doesn't want this and it will weaken you. Unclean spirits have emotions and so do we. Remember, you are casting out a spirit that has already died and has entered someone else's body to cause them sickness and destruction.

The entire pattern of unclean spirits is the destruction of all mankind. They are not leading you to a fairyland or to heaven because they cannot. The entire spiritual world on this earth is extremely cold, meaning without any love. Hate, anger, and evil are the orders of the day for them. There are no saved spirits in this world. All saved persons go straight to heaven after they die.

The unclean spirits of unsaved persons are under directives from fallen angels to make you sick, pervert your thoughts, and if possible possess your body. In the book, **The Sequel**, this subject is expanded. Don't be foolish and allow unclean spirits to enter you. They enter you when you sin, so try your best to obey the Word. If you fall and sin, ask God to forgive you immediately and ask the Holy Spirit to teach you and guide you to righteousness. Sometimes it takes years to change, but you must try your best.

The "command" is always firmly directed at the unclean spirit(s). Sometimes, I get criticized for swearing, when I am exorcising. Yes, they often get to me through the tremendous harm they have caused the person. How would you feel if the cause of your love one's lameness is some spirit trying to kill them? All casting outs of unclean spirits is serious. Always be serious towards the goal. Because of this, I am not nice but very tough.

The unclean spirits know why I am there, they even try to intercept me before I get to someone's house. They try to enter me or cause some problem with someone around me. This entire spirit business is very deadly. They are out for keeps and so am I. They have tormented people, who have no way to fight back. This book places a nuclear gun in your hands. You will become the tormentor and the unclean spirits will become the tormented. Future encounters by you will always be devastating for them. **Be strong and of good courage—Joshua 1:5-9.**

Now with this background about the "Command", the next step is to know what to "command." The following should be helpful to understand what to command:

1. All commands must be strong.

2. Effective commands are directed at the unclean spirit, which has positioned his/herself in the person to be spoken to. Often there is more than one unclean spirit in a person. From experience there is always a leading spirit who has dominance over all other spirits in the person. Casting out of the leading spirit normally permits the casting out of all other spirits. By spiritual discernment, one can see the unclean spirit(s) take position in the face of the person. The countenance changes as a new unclean spirit takes position to speak. It is possible to actually see the person whom you are speaking to.

3. The sequential context of the commands should follow this outline: find out who you are talking to; how they died previously; what sickness they brought into the persons body; and why are they there—then cast them out immediately

4. All commands must be associated with the binding force of the Word of God and the Name of Jesus

For example: In the Name of Jesus, I command you to… I break all your power and bind you helpless against this person, never to enter again, by the Name of Jesus; In the Name of Jesus I command you to be loose from this person and never to enter again…

Again, be strong and of good courage. Someone's life may depend on your strength. Command is not praying. Again, Command is not praying. Don't pray in front of an unclean spirit trying to kill you. Tell him/her to take a hike! Sometimes, I just scream at them— "get out!" They leave. There is a statute in the leper colony in Asia. It is an angel stepping on the head of an unclean spirit and sticking a spear into the unclean spirit. Exorcism is one of several things: your angels casting out the spirits; the Holy Spirit in you casting out the spirits; or the Holy Spirit in the Word coming out of your mouth as the Sword of the Spirit. During this section of the book, there is no powering up of faith. The Word must have the Holy Spirit power to be a Sword of the Spirit. It is not how you dress or look or how oratory you can be, but is the power of God in you.

Chapter X
Participation of The Holy Spirit

The communion of the Holy Spirit in your life is extremely critical. Without it you are not spiritual. Many who state within one breath that they are spiritual, often do not understand what is spiritual. To be spiritual, under basic Christian terminology, means to have all the gifts of the Holy Spirit working in your life. Do you have the gifts of healing, tongue [speech], interpretation, faith, miracles, prophecy, knowledge, discernment, and wisdom? Do you have at least three to four of them? If you don't, then I don't understand what you mean by being spiritual? "I don't make any bones about it, most of the Christians claiming to be spiritual are really not."

There is no shame to it, they haven't allowed the Holy Spirit to operate in their lives and bodies, nor has the seminary taught exorcism. If you would like to become spiritual, then you must yield to the Holy Spirit. Learn to let the Holy Spirit come into your heart and body. He is not only gentle, but He will exalt you. He created you and brings a "full plate" to your table. Allow only the Holy Spirit to enter in you and none other. Any spirit that exists in this world and not in heaven's paradise is an unclean spirit.

Most people cannot notion the concept and idea of letting God come into their lives, as if there was some secret they were keeping from God. He can even tell you how many hairs are on your head. Even I cannot count them. Can you? The unsaved lives a life of total ignorance. In one sad exorcism, I met one of my family members. I asked her, "Why didn't you come to God?" She answered in words that burned in my soul— "no one taught me." Don't let this be your loved one's legacy.

The gifts of the Holy Spirit remain with the Holy Spirit. It is His power and it also is the Holy Spirit who releases and operates through you. We don't have the gifts to put into our pockets and walk around all day with. With man being so weak and feeble, it would be a potential disaster awaiting to happen. The great ministers of our times have anointing of the Holy Spirit. To become strong in the Spirit or to walk in the Spirit, one must ask Him to commune with us. Ask for the gifts, in great abundance. Lord, fill me with the gifts of the Holy Spirit in the fullness of the Godhead or without measure. Most ministers pray this type of prayer prior to the conduct of services.

We must have direct communion with the Holy Spirit prior to any deliverance or service. The purpose of church is to grow spiritually in the Holy Spirit, who will in turn teach us all things. Many of us, profess to learn the Word of God for our lives as a result of church. At some point, the Christian's spirit will become hungry for the fellowship of the Holy Spirit.

To be in a spiritual walk with the Holy Spirit is more important than scriptural understanding. Holy Spirit understanding is more important than scriptural understanding. Why? The Holy Spirit is God. Let God teach and commune with you. Yes, there are some real smart ministers, but wouldn't you rather learn from God than from God's creation? Many people worship ministers and many ministers like it, but it is entirely wrong. That is not the point of church, that we become the disciples of men, but only of God. There is no person inclusive in the Lord, nor does any one person have the wisdom or knowledge that cannot be outgrown by another person.

The Holy Spirit is whom we all should commune with daily. If you don't have a daily life with the Holy Spirit, then during those time you need Him, may He be there for you. Let Him lead you. "I don't know how." First, praise Him, worship Him as God and then commune with Him. Before you know it you will find Him there in your heart! You can see things, people cannot see; know things people cannot know; understand things people cannot understand.

I once was criticized by someone who stole my manuscripts from me, "that @#!* walks and talks with God" in a sarcastic manner. That was quite a compliment, thank you. Learn to yield to the Holy Spirit. Just await for Him to come into your heart. Pray in reverence, pray in desire for communion with Him, and ask Him to teach you all things. He will respond to you.

Once the Holy Spirit begins to move your heart, use your mouth. Let me say it again, use your mouth. Then you will see the blessings of the Lord. Often, the Holy Spirit would use my mouth and say something to someone. A 50-year-old man came to my home one day and I turned to him and say one sentence to him, he fell to the ground and cried. Only he knew what was his deepest secret. God also knew. I would meet people whom I never met in my life and all of a sudden start to tell them about their youth and how they have misunderstandings about the bible/God.

One day a young man came to my home and asked to stay there for three weeks. I never met him before and after 10 minutes of listening to him how the Holy Spirit baptized him with fire. I stopped him and asked him why does he still take drugs? He vehemently denied it, until I said, "you took drugs two weeks ago." He bowed his head in shame and said he was sorry. He actually got scared and avoided meeting with me again.

One night I was praying and a face of a man with one eye appeared. "Lord, show me who this is?" The face changed and wow! It was my friend. One month later, he came to my office, I asked him, "One month ago, you prayed against me, why?" He vehemently denied it. I said, "Yes you did." Then he bowed his head and said I was angry with you. I turned to him and said, "In three weeks you will lose everything you own." He lost everything in two weeks and became afraid to see me again. During these words of knowledge and prophecies, I had no idea I was going to say something to this effect. I spoke to four different people that the Lord was going to take them before they died. The Lord wanted them to get their houses in order and it was their blessing.

Are you afraid to become spiritual? It's quite the opposite. You know that God is there with you, what is there to be afraid of? Even the spirits know you. The spiritual gifts are so gentle and natural, that it is hard to understand. But once you know who He is, you can begin to understand the whole process and watch it unfold.

One of my laying of hands resulted in a couple freed of cancer. It was so strong to the couple they both rejoiced in their healing as soon as they got off their knees. When I laid hands on their heads, I felt nothing. In the Philippines, a young woman was knocked down fifteen feet away, just by pointing a finger at her. It was so strong, I almost had to look at my finger to see if it was smoking. People had fallen down just by yelling at them. When you see the faces of deliverance it is so happy. I think God is very happy when His children are delivered. God may be laughing at me, but it's OK, I know His works and He is glorious. Do it again, Lord.

Chapter XI
Satanic Hirarchy

Unless you have a strong understanding of the Satanic hierarchy, you are incapable of fighting any warfare. How is it possible to fight a war against an enemy that you have little or no knowledge? If you can't even see spirits, then just how are you going to give them a knock out punch?

Let me say this, if you are so charged up as most "spirit filled churches portend and you going to punch Satan in the nose and your going out to look for him, then be sure you have a paid up life insurance policy in effect. It is a reprehensible and a fully irresponsible act of church leaders to claim to be spiritual and lead members of the flock to fight a satanic war without real knowledge.

If you belong to a church that has such courageous leaders, my advise to you is to get out of that church before you and your family/friends gets wiped out! The satanic hierarchy is formidable!

Whenever, I meet ministers from Africa, I normally criticize them for deliberately misleading US pastors who go to Africa to bring the word of God to them. There is nothing wrong with bringing the word, but most US pastors who go to other foreign lands, especially, Africa, Caribbean, South America, depart the USA with a sense of dedicated missions and a high feeling that they are bringing some new good news of the gospel to the ignorant of these lands. God bless each and every missionary, but there are some who feel the superior spiritual purpose of such missions. Isn't this a common occurrence?

The U.S. pastor has superior spiritual knowledge he wants to share in these far-removed foreign lands. Can you imagine teaching African pastors about spirits? They know more about spirits than most U.S. pastor will ever learn. The spirit world is more real to them than the secular world. Sometimes we form a false premise upon which we build our knowledge and lives. What is good for the pastor is good for everyone else?

If you have a chance to seriously ask an African pastor about spirits, have him teach you and you will gain more from that conversation than watching a pastor try to lay empty hands on empty heads. It is the pastor's responsibility to lead the flock correctly to grow and be strong, not to be led to a slaughter. Perhaps, this misrepresentation is a cause for the exodus of many from the churches. Almost everyone circulates amongst the churches until they find a church that they feel comfortable. Remember, I said comfortable, not find the Comforter.

Unless you grasp the full meaning of this book, you're a "sitting duck." The purpose of the book is to change you from the "tormented" to the "tormentor." The contents of this book will change your life completely and open your eyes as to what is going on in the world. Do not play with the principles in this book as it represents power from God, not from you.

Having read hundreds of books about the scriptures, Jesus, Christianity—the best book that gives an eye-witness account of the complete satanic hierarchy is Rev. Howard O. Pittman's book—**Demons**. Pastor Pittman spent 26 years as a law enforcement officer and as a pastor. Pastor Pittman had a death experience in 8/3/79 and was shown the satanic hierarchy. This hierarchy is consistent with the experiential knowledge and patterns of actions by "unclean spirits" of the author.

OVERVIEW: There is an absence of love, kindness, mercy, truth, and justice in the satanic world. It is the very opposite of what we understand heaven to be. Nothing of earth can resemble this spirit world. It is a very explicit spiritual world that has a hierarchy structure based upon: strength; misery; hate; greed; anger; war; and deception. It is very well structured and has been in place since mankind's existence. There is darkness and extreme coldness of heart.

There are 5 levels of satanic activities, they are:

1. *Warring Angelic level*—territories of powerful angelic beings, with princes to over see all the activities within their principalities. They clearly know what is happening within their principalities. They know everything about you and your weaknesses. War is the by-product of the activities in each principality.

2. *Man-Like spirits*—this level, the angelic activity involves commerce, wealth, riches, selfishness, greed, deals with economies of the world. Is the 2nd in command after the warring angels.

3. *Part-Man, Part-animal*—deals with false religions, occult, satanic worship, and reincarnation.

4. *Mystery spirits*—deals with "unclean spirit" activities in humans, such as sickness, diseases, possessions, infirmities, and afflictions.

5. *Frog-Like spirit*—despicable spirits in ugly shapes, stalking people, awaiting to enter them through the face, afflicting the sovereign will of people, such as "desires" and lusts.

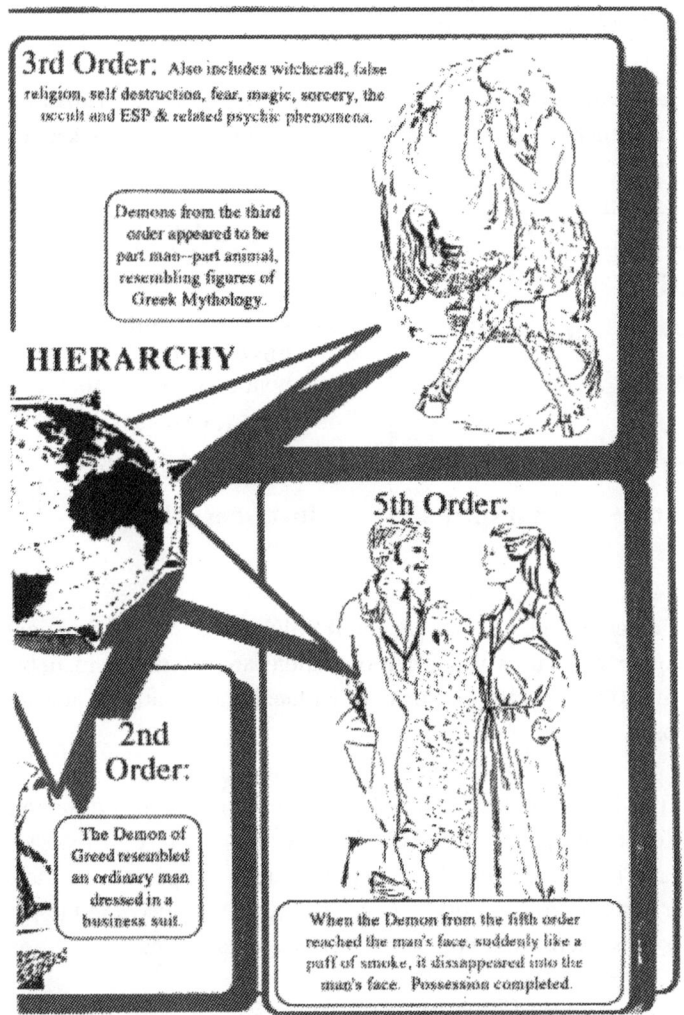

The above pictures/drawings are reprinted with permission from Mr. Howard O. Pittman, author of **Demons: An Eye-Witness Account**. (1980's)

Satanic Hierarchy

Ephesians 6:12—For we wrestle not against flesh and blood, but against principalities, against powers, against the rulers of darkness of this world, against spiritual wickedness in high places.

ENTITY	POSITION	PURPOSE
Warring angel	rulers	rule over principalities
Power angel	principalities	power over economics, governments
Man/animal Spirit	wicked spirits	perversion of religions
Mystery Spirit	unclean spirits	sickness, diseases, oppression, possession
Frog-like Spirit	animal spirits	lust, sensualities

The Warring Angel, Power Angel, and Man/animal Spirit have specific functions toward large areas or countries in the world. Their operations are external to man, but appear to come from mankind. Specific persons are targeted and greatly influenced to carry out their purposes.

Mystery Spirits and frog-like spirits enter people to alter their thoughts, direction, health, and create dysfunctional personalities within a person. Because of their secretive nature to remain innocuous, they're most dangerous to persons without comprehension of their activities or purpose. Upon disclosure, they become the target of torment by Christians exercising the **Word of God** against them.

Angelic warfare can be great, but specifically directed angelic power against these angels/spirits is very effective. As Jesus commanded the violent waves to subside and the fierce winds to be quiet, they obeyed. By observation, there is little directed angelic warfare against different religions in the world. This is from the spiritual ignorance of the Christian world.

Angelic warfare and **intervention** against the unclean spirits and frog-like spirits are very effective. To control your own life and to stay away from harm's way, angelic intervention is essential. After one has defeated the enemies, they must help and fight for the brethren.

Summary: The woes of this world could be directly related back to the activities of this hierarchy. The woes include: war, strife, evil, lies, sickness, diseases, cults, perversions, and no hope for a future for mankind. It would be no less than a comprehensive hierarchy to pervert all of mankind. It has been going on for thousands of years.

Do you think you can go out and look to punch Satan in the nose, without getting "hit" yourself? From what your church and your own knowledge of the spirit world has given you, are you prepared to fight? What are your weapons? How do you use it? What happens, if the enemy commences to destroy your loved ones around you, before you get out the door?

Have you adequately protected your loved ones? Do you know how to stop the human carnage that this satanic hierarchy has been purposed and created? May the serious minded Christians understand what I am trying to say. Look at all human misery. God never purposed such misery and suffering—it comes from Satan.

Occasionally, I have to shut the television off, because what I see is a well-structured, hierarchy based upon the destruction of all flesh. Keep in mind, man has been Satan's trap. Because he was cursed of God to hate the seed of the woman (**Gen 3:15**) and the seed of the woman (all mankind or flesh) was going to defeat him. Satan has an enormous hatred of all mankind, this is why he has intended for all mankind, even those who would even worship him, to a life of misery and suffering. Doesn't matter whether you like him or not, he has the intent to destroy all mankind.

Wake up, he hasn't stopped on putting you in his sights to target you for destruction. That's why even evil persons, non-Christians, atheists, liars, whoremongers, good Samaritans, devil worshippers, psychics, illiterates, idiots, intellectuals, and the rest of mankind has been entangled in his hierarchy. There is probably nothing you can tell the former anointed cherub that shielded God from creation and possesses perfect wisdom, that would change his mind.

He has been judged before you and I was borne. He was defeated by Jesus, who came in the flesh (God with us, the Messiah, the Savior, the Word made flesh) to defeat Satan and become the sacrifice for our sins, so that we can have our spirit made clean, enabling us to go to heaven and be the children of God, to rule with Jesus in an everlasting kingdom, that will commence with the final act of God to expel all rebellion into the lake of fire.

The problem is not hierarchy but the lack of knowledge by Christians to fight against such a system (**Hosea 4:6**). Yes, the enemy is tough, but Jesus didn't leave us helpless to be defeated by someone He has already defeated.

Do you think that God left us for the slaughter? Do you think that your church would leave you for the slaughter? Where are our weapons? Where are our warriors? Who is instructing us to defend ourselves against the onslaught? Since it is a spiritual warfare, how do we become spiritual? Who is to teach us to become spiritual? Answer these questions for yourselves and know clearly where you stand!

Fundamentalism has reversed the Christian's growth towards spirituality. A non-spiritual church or pastor cannot help you for the warfare. Spiritual gifts and growth have not been clearly explained by the bible. Part of your salvation is the "born again by the Holy Spirit." This means your spiritual warfare, should you be plagued by demons, is your own problem.

Hear this well, read **Mark 16:15–18—and He said to them, Go ye into all the world and preach the gospel to every creature. He that believeth and is baptized shall be saved; but he that believeth not is damned. And these signs shall follow**

them that believe; In my name they shall cast out devils; they shall speak with new tongues; They shall take up serpents; and if they drink any deadly thing, it shall not hurt them; they shall lay hands on the sick, and they shall recover. It is my basic position that unless these signs follow your belief in Jesus, you may want to rethink your position in Christ as to where you are. If you are an ardent church-going Christian, then examine how the church has instructed you in this Christian walk.

This verse in **Mark** is very important in your understanding as how these things are to interact in your life. **Verse 20** is critical?**and they went forth and preached everywhere, the Lord working with them, and confirming the word with signs following. Amen.** Who does the signs, the same person who has been doing them all along—Jesus, at the right hand of the Father interceding for you and all of us. Here is the benchmark of those who believe. Since Jesus said it, do you believe it or has someone redefined the word to you to mean something else—it couldn't have been made simpler.

In every level, Jesus has countered every act of evil. The truth will set us free. Free from what? What does truth really set us free from? Here is the partial list—every lie, false premise, from any authority other than God, from every accusation, from every sin, sickness, disease, and from evil itself. Now, what is left? By our own finite knowledge, we can easily conclude that for every evil there can be an opposing good. Is that what God has done? I say that overlooks the; point that God is Omniscience, Omnipresent, Omnipower, Holy, Almighty, King of Kings, Lord of Lords, the Creator, and a few more descriptive attributes of God Himself. The spread, folks, from *#1* to *#2* is the distance from heaven to hell. {You will or you won't get into heaven.}

There is no comparability; yet, we are led to believe the grandiose frustrated dreams of a creature as having the ability over the Creator! We tell ourselves that we are the masters of our own destiny, folks, should this be the case, we would be living in hell within 100 years. Beauty, brightness, power, and pride can be defined as a human value that when compared to the attributes of the Creator of all things, then truth loses it relationship to mankind.

Place this thought against a back ground of: creating the heavens and the earth; creating all creatures and living things; taking care of the different types of creatures in the very depths of the oceans; to ensuring the birds are designed to fly; and having the Word become flesh—then match this against the five levels of the satanic hierarchy as previously described. Who do you think will be the winner? Who have you placed as the winner in your life? Have you allowed a creature to take control of your life? Have you allowed the Creator to take over your life to give you a life without corruption?

1. **Warring Angels** are only one-third of the angelic creation. The other two-thirds of angels are in heaven and on this earth waging a war for you. **Hebrew 1:13-14—But to which of the angels said He at any time, Sit on My Right hand, until I make thine enemies thy footstool? Are they not all ministering spirits, sent forth to minister for them who shall be the heirs of salvation?** Hasn't God fought wars and battles for His people, throughout the Old Testament? Do you think He has stopped since Jesus appeared? Who do you think will put away once and for all eternity all rebellion at the end of the millennium, by sending fire from heaven?—God.

2. **Man-Like Spirit**—the economies of the world have been under severe stress from influences and interactions with other nations. The severity of economic destabilization is similar in impact to that of a war. Recognition and availability of a nation's currency is the determinant for prosperity or poverty. Historic greed of few has kept the many in abject poverty. The rights of kings have been enforced by military might. It reduces down to a rule of force. Run away inflation (over-printing of money) deteriorates the needed purchasing power of the citizenry; while, fiscal controls of monetary policies are far removed from most political influence. You want to bet, it is the eye of the economic storms!

In today's world, the "new world order" represents an order of monetary control such as G-7 and not the ideologies of differing forms of governments, the few remain the administrators of the many... The EMU (European Monetary Union) is going to play a decisive role in world power. By 2002, it stands to become the world's most dominant economic power, with 15 nations combining its monetary power as a single bloc. The Euro dollar will become larger than the U.S. dollar and world dominance of the "international exchange medium" will shift to the Euro dollar as well as the economic base of international commerce. The pivot nation is to be Great Britain in 2002.

The U.S. was sold out by its own legislators and executives with the formation of WTO, then a series of international agreements that diffuses power from the U.S. My own opinion is it becomes a necessary shift to support the emergence of the antichrist. The economic power was always in Europe for hundreds of years. So what has changed? Look at the people we have running the government, does any one care?

Peace—a passive rallying point for differing governments is not a common "overriding" factor as to why governments cooperate with each other, but their alliances are easily overshadowed by the enormous efforts of every government to stabilize their monetary prowess within a global forum; it is by invitation only.

The depth of the power of a nation is the extension of its monetary base within the world. Within each nation the central banking infrastructure and its role to other nations and the U.S. dollar have become the most powerful resource of that nation.

Since the times of Andrew Jackson, the autonomous nature of central banks have shown clear evidence of a silent, but overriding power, within every nation. This silent force, which rules international currency, shall rise to power during the reign of the antichrist to be the false prophet who will control the world's commerce. The mark of the beast shall be given as a requirement to buy and sell. By this time it will become apparent that the commerce is a symbol of the antichrist. Until this "future new world order" becomes established, we can observe the shift from military force to political force to monetary force as the controlling factor of power—all the while the final destination of power will become the commerce base of nations.

The activities of this man-like spirit will be far reaching, to deliver the commerce of the world into the hands of the false prophet. The final destruction of the future Babylon will be a symbol of the end of the false prophet who will be thrown into the Lake of Fire. For those Christians who have placed the value and purpose of money/business over all other values, may they understand that their efforts has been a manipulation by the Man-Like spirits of the satanic hierarchy. Having understood this, does the personal values taught to us, that wealth is power, becomes an obstacle to personal Christian growth? Wealth in allegiance with political and military power has been orchestrated for hundreds of years.

3. ***Half-Man/Half-Animal spirits***—the breadth of what people believe in their lives can be attributable to this level. Within Christianity itself, there are thousands of different representations of Jesus. Can you tell which is the true gospel? The theological seminaries have become far removed from spirituality. Can the "clone" religions be separated behind a mask of subjective and analytical treatise, but different, interpretations of the scriptures? The selection criteria for a church/religion is subjective at best. The parable of the sower is the best description of Christianity—about 25% will have the word of God implanted in their lives—enough to allow the Lord to grant salvation as an act of grace. What happens to the others? The numerous non-Christian religions are very appealing, since they enable interaction with spiritual forces. Deception by this satanic hierarchy is considerable and pervasive. An overview of the origins of all the major religions and their purposeful detraction from Christianity is an indication as to the power of this level. Within all religions are serious and sincere people who believe to the point of dying for their beliefs. With this in mind, the individualistic depth and influence by demonic activities covers all religions. None are excluded and exempt from being called a satanic cult by the other religions.

4. ***Mystery Spirit***—it is with firm conviction that this level best describes the role of "unclean spirits" depicted by the scriptures. The act of incarnation into the body of another person seems most logically to be the "spirit" of another person who has died and did not go to heaven. The "unclean spirit" in the scriptures, does not represent a fallen angel, but the spirit of an "unsaved" person after death. Despite the claims of famous evangelists, pastors and ministers—that the "unclean spirit" is a demon is only partially accurate.

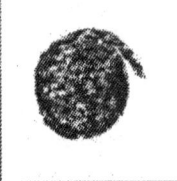

The Asian name of the "unclean spirit" is Gee-shin, creature of the nervous system. The travel within a person's body is along the nerves. During one of our church meetings, our evangelists asked about what an unclean spirit looks like. They didn't believe that something like that could enter a Christian. Without any hesitation, I asked the sister of the evangelist to raise her arm. Everyone's mouth went wide open, when they all saw a very dark shadow moving back and forth along her arm. I did not know personally whether the spirit would show up on her arm or not, but I was moved by the Holy Spirit to speak out.

The activity level by unclean spirits is very substantial in peoples' lives—as they enter people to: make them sick; possess them; alter their lives in order to "induce personality traits of the spirit's former life" and also to even kill the body before salvation can take hold. The term unclean spirit is so misrepresented that it is difficult to know who and what is right. The best description of an unclean spirit is in **2 Esdras 7:69–103**. Nowhere else does a description occur in the scriptures.

There are very few or no training programs in the United States for ministers or laity to learn scriptural healing. There are only few places in the world that provide effective training. The pastors at these training academies are very strong in knowledge of the scriptures. Almost all have powerful spiritual gifts of the Holy Spirit. All have the spiritual discernment gift. To have the discernment gift in reading the scriptures is to re-establish all doctrinal understanding. Some of these pastors have churches with more than 20,000 members and they are able to discern the unclean spirits. They can discern illness inside of you 10,000 miles away. They can see spirits inside and outside a person. My very dear pastor friend has people running away from him or passing out if they come near him.

This book is written to warn all Christians and to educate them about the origin and activities of the unclean spirits. The total spiritual life of an unclean spirit is 120 years old. (**Gen. 6:3**) After the attainment of the 120 years, the spirit of a person who is unsaved or the spirit of a person who is not clean by the blood of Jesus on the cross, goes to Sheol, the place for the unsaved souls to await judgment.

The spirit of a person having once left its body at death is separated from that body. The spirits of the dead persons are able to "enter the bodies" of people and they do it for many reasons. As Jesus cast out the legion of unclean spirits in the Maniac of Gedara, the spirits talked back to Jesus. The person they entered became as crazy to the world. The craziness within this person was not his craziness but of those whom have entered him.

Everyone has had unclean spirits enter their bodies at some time or another. Outside the body, the unclean spirits feel cold and are unable to act out a personality in a physical world. Once entered into someone, the unclean spirits seek to force their personalities upon the person. People with distinctive personality changes, multiple personalities, and sickness have unclean spirits in their bodies. One of the most dangerous things an unclean spirit can do, is the very act of creation of thought patterns within a person.

People believe it is them, but in reality, it was the unclean spirit, seeking to act out their lives again in someone else's body. There are many instances of split personalities, who are nothing more than the incarnation of unclean spirits into them. The second level of danger is what the unclean spirit brings with them at entry. Many bring sickness and disease.

The most predominant trait about unclean spirits within a person is the personality attributes. Keep in mind that often men enter women and women enter men. If you expand this thought further, one can see how men would take on female personalities?once a female unclean spirit enters his body. Can you see how this relates to what is happening in this world?

The claimants who declare their own sexual gender to the world because "somehow" they were "borne" in the wrong body of the wrong sex—nothing could be further from the truth! Expand this revelation to the gay world and the resulting impact will be no less than nuclear! Exactly how is it possible that a person with an unclean spirit within them, seeking a doctor who heals physical ailments and definitely non-spiritual causes, can ever be healed? Do you think spirits will react to medicine, surgery, science; how about a diploma?

How is it possible that a psychiatrist/psychologist can ever expect to bring a cure to someone who has a spirit problem? Should the cure be by someone who can diagnose and remove the problem? It would seem practical. Now just how would you heal a spirit problem? Do you go to someone who has no power to deliver?

God stated in the bible that He is the God that healeth thee. With this in mind, can other gods heal a spiritual problem? Why or why not? Can a Buddhist heal a spirit problem? Can a fundamentalist church heal a spirit problem? Who exactly does the healing? God. How? By His word.

This level of satanic hierarchy will be the central theme of this book.

5. ***Frog-Like creatures***—the last of the hierarchy are these animal and part creature-like spirits that enter people through their face. They stalk people awaiting apparently for a vulnerable moment, then they enter the face of a person. Moments of lust, anger, pride, hate, greed, and evil provide the keys for these creatures to enter people. Perhaps, these ungodly attitudes are gateways between the desires of the flesh and this world that emanate from the inner being of people to their conscious minds and their flesh.

Lust is often overwhelming. The senses are distorted and a physical attraction becomes difficult to control. We are distinct from animals because we have the ability to reason. By what we reason, becomes our understanding to our fellow man. People who happen to meet, just don't fall all over themselves, but some people characterize this behavior as love. Is it really love? Can love really be the common point of relationships at first glance? Is it possible?

The best of relationships are built on strong, understood, and well-defined common bonds. Then, just what exactly is this "love" impulse? From experience as an exorcist—whenever you are "pulled" or "pushed" there is a high probability that an unclean spirit is inducing you to act. We are not animals and our reasoning should best dictate our actions and understanding.

We have all seen animals in the acts of lust and sex. If we allow ourselves to behave in such like manners, we would be no better than animals ourselves. The next time we "give" affections of trust, care, unselfishness, and patience to someone we love, you will realize that what these moments of lust are.

If someone distorts your body's "erogenous zones", your physiological composure will react. An evil spirit within your body can imitate feelings and desires that have nothing to do with any real affection or what you yourselves would feel under circumstances controlled by you.

Think about it, if an evil spirit assimilates stimulation of your erogenous zones, all without any love, trust, real affection or care, would you really describe such intrusions of your privacy as real love? Is it raw lust? Do you know the difference? There are many criminals who end up in prison, because they did not know why they committed such heinous crimes. First, they were not the real motivating force behind the act and second, they really didn't know it was not them.

If you have a frog-like creature enter you in the face and travel along your nervous system, what do you think is going to happen to you? If it entered your loved ones, would it make you mad? Don't get mad, get even!

In summary, the 5 levels of satanic activities are very well organized and extremely destructive. How can we overcome and defeat such activities in your life? Remember **Mark 16**, if you believe then you should be able to—cast out devils. God has already given us the power to defend ourselves and have victory over these activities. If you can understand this book, you will become the "tormentor" and the satanic hierarchy will become the "tormented."

If you don't understand or misapply the knowledge given to you by this book, you will remain the tormented. We are "sitting ducks" unless we know how to overcome these activities in our lives. It will be necessary to write books to elaborate and expand upon the areas covered in this chapter.

For understanding, let us embark upon an unselfish journey to bring real healing, deliverance, and free the afflicted. May some readers advance themselves in this knowledge and become a fountain of life to many. As I enjoy watching TV deliverance ministries and understand how God has given to some precious ministers great gifts of healing, faith, discernment and miracles—let the words of the Lord be made full by your faith and actions.

If you are not gifted by God then be blessed by God's Word and remember it is Jesus who confirms His Word with signs and wonders. What you need is to believe in Him, that the Lord will confirm His Word with signs and wonders. After your first real deliverance, observe the face of the delivered person, it will tell you the power and love of His Word.

To become expedient in exorcism it takes considerable effort and resolve on your part to be determined to wage a war of your faith, with scriptural understanding, against the unclean spirit's right to be in the person's body. The first few initial encounters will tell you how strong they are and their resolve to destroy people's lives.

Chapter XII
Traits of The Unclean Spirits

The description in **2 Esdras 7** presents the spiritual world itself to the unsaved. Shock, disbelief, fear, jealousy, and real understanding become a reality for those who have just died. Absent from their bodies they feel extreme coldness, amongst a judged hierarchy of hatred, lust, evil, anger, deceit, and violence. The final realization of the existence of a real God and a real devil, whom they have disregarded during their lives, now becomes the truth from which they cannot be set free, but will remain until that time of judgment by the Lord.

The forced servitude by which they must now enjoin, will become their "unclean spirit life." There is no place to run or hide. The evil which they have accepted into their lives now is the only tool which they can use to express themselves. Without the incarnate nature of unclean spirits, there would be no further ties to a physical world. They had their chance and they blew it.

The satanic hierarchy is based upon strength as the determinant of authority. Satan's previous position in heaven reflected such demarcations of authority and has now become the separating factor between differing levels of activities. From exorcisms, the unclean spirits have indicated they are supervised "forcefully" by angels. The torment even within the satanic hierarchy continues. There are beatings by angels on unclean spirits. It's not an orgy or beer party, its hell!

To survive in this earth bound spiritual world of judged creatures, they must "fall into place" by becoming one of them. The very evil, deception, lies, hatred, jealousy, anger which they were once constrained by a society of "good" and "evil" people—

has now become pervasive. This side without God and His precepts to guide them no more. The "god" of this world has taken another unsaved person into his fold to continue to do his works.

To excel in this spirit world, you have to become mean and do all that of the father of all lies, the murderer from the beginning, the one who understand the depth of power himself and who fell from grace. To enter this world, fear embraces one and then by design, becomes the tormentor of fear and deceit for those still in the physical world.

The underlying unique ability of unclean spirits from the rest of the satanic hierarchy is that he/she once possessed a body. They lived in a body previously and apparently have the ability to "re-enter" a body even with someone else possessing it. The incorporeal nature of the unclean spirit can allow many even thousands of unclean spirits to enter and remain within a body. When Jesus commanded the maniac of Gedara, who was there—the spirits answered, "legion" meaning thousands of unclean spirits within one person.

Once inside a person's body, the spirits feel warm and can evoke their personalities again through the person. Inside a person's body, the unclean spirits commences a process and program of: oppression; depression; repression; and finally possession. The mental institutions are full of people who have substantiated this pattern. The prisons are full of people who have succumbed to being victimized by possession and demonic activities.

If you don't know what it is and cannot figure it out, then put a new name on a new dementia and file it. Reason cannot free these people, someone's prior sexual inhibitions cannot free them, a college degree cannot free these people; but, the Spirit of the Lord can. Our judicial system does not understand nor has anyone proven the existence of the unclean spirit, except some ministers. There are people incarcerated because of serious possession by demonic spirits acting as the "thoughts" of the person.

People are as diverse as the grains of sand on the beaches. The variance of intellect, ignorance, comprehension, perception, humor, sensitivity, emotions, and understanding is reflective of the breadth of responses that emanates from the unclean spirits encountered. Despite this potentially wide variance, a pattern emerges to define the consensus of the responses.

The fields of psychiatry and psychology have programs that treat persons that are possessed. There are volumes of reasons that these treatment programs are not curing the cause of the problem. Instead of a chastisement of these fields, since there are sincere and serious people in it, I would rather opt for a series of constructive resolutions.

Many of these resolutions could bring proper and true redirection to the multitude of "mysteries" that have alluded root causation of the many, many mental disorders within these fields. Don't get me wrong about my strong feelings about these fields, since my mother suffered great harm for years under these professions.

How do you treat a problem that is a spirit within a person? Do you reason? Medicate? Apply electroshock therapy? Perform surgery on the brain? Would a bunch of expensive sessions on a couch talking about your sexual life help? Is it possible to cure the problem without understanding the causation?

Can I tell them it is a dead spirit that is causing the problem? Folks, forgive my strong questions, but isn't that what it is all about? Silent tears fell within me at the joy of the family of my dear friend when the surgeons of a great hospital told them that all the cancer is gone. Six months later it came back to consume her. My thesis is this: if the cause of the disease is not severed, then the disease remains. Her love for us in the ministry remains with us and is one of the reasons, this book is written.

I am willing to undertake a "scientific study" with the fields mentioned herein to prove the veracity of the contents of this book. The mysteries of homosexuality, death, spirit intrusions, and activities can be resolved. I would like for some members of the clergy to join with me. The legal profession should be advised of the study and results. I would do this for the millions of souls incarcerated and tormented, they have no hope or time.

It would be appropriate to discuss the normal nature of unclean spirits, but the purpose of this book is to offer the victory over unclean spirits, not to drift into a social debate of man's tradition. It is the author's intent to make you the "tormentor" and no longer the "tormented." You may disagree with me, but the difference between the two is your life or your death.

You have to know how to throw a "knock-out" punch. We are not here to placate the pride of mankind; but, these facts could be substantiated and the judicial and mental health groups should incorporate this knowledge. The truth shall set them free.

The unclean spirits that we encounter will carry a constant remnant of their death as well as the personalities of their former lives. If someone had died from a brain tumor, then the symptomatic traits of a brain tumor emerges from that unclean spirit within the body of another person. These traits become a "give-away" that there is another spirit within. Personality traits, habits, desires, behavior, and other "out-of-personality" behavior can literally describe the unclean spirits within.

You must keep in mind that these unclean spirits cannot act out their personalities without being inside a living body. If they are outside the body, they have no way to impress themselves within a physical world. A world lost to them until the judgment.

Ignorance, lack of focus, seriousness, and submissive behavior are some the traits of unclean spirits. Despite the well-structured satanic hierarchy, the overwhelming "dis-interest" of the unclean spirits are also the order of the day. Only in the cases of possession, are the unclean spirits serious. From the number of exorcisms performed, many unclean spirits are "hiding" them-selves within the bodies of people they knew previously.

Hospitals, funeral homes, cemeteries are the places with active manifestation of unclean spirits. Employees of these places often "pick up" the unclean spirits, only to receive manifestations of personality changes and diseases.

Diseases are brought in a person's body through the entry of unclean spirits bringing sickness and diseases. Most sickness and diseases are spiritually derived. The actual exorcisms by Jesus, whereby he cast out the unclean spirits, then all manner of sickness and diseases departed. The actual act of healing was the expulsion of the unclean spirit and the sickness/disease it brought in. In the many exorcisms conducted, when the unclean spirit was cast out, the person was healed of their sickness and disease.

Luke 8:2—and certain women, which had been healed of evil spirits and infirmities, Mary called Magdalene, out of whom went seven devils. The New Testament is full of examples of healing by Jesus—all related to having the evil spirits cast out, then the sickness left. It is wrong, both factually and scripturally to assert that sickness and diseases are only physically inherent, instead of—derived from a spirit source.

This author does not downplay the role of medicine in your life but in the absence of your knowledge of the spirit world and how it really has been functioning, your own physical well-being is subject to your own understanding and the source of sickness.

Unsaved people that have died from many kinds of sicknesses and diseases, carry the trauma of these sicknesses and/or diseases with them to the spirit world. An unsaved person who died in a car accident, which cut off their legs would maintain vivid memories of the pain and disability of the severed limbs, even as a spirit.

Upon the entry into another living person, the unclean spirit would act out the pain and trauma of their former demise to the person whom they have entered. The unsuspecting person would suffer this anguish, without any knowledge of the reason why. Every person reading this book, knows of someone who has: the feeling of some one inside of them; feels pain, but cannot find the causation; experiences out-of-character behaviors that is foreign to them; and often feel "pushed" or "pulled" to do something. What are the causes of these behavioral inconsistencies?

Many unclean spirits have the tendency to remain stealthy and somewhat dormant. There are unclean spirits that are totally confused, ignorant as even to what and where they are. Often the spirits of children remain subject to everyone and everything they encounter. Despite the environment and circumstance to grow older, they literally remain somewhat child-like despite their age from birth. They often remain within a person for many years, without "exerting" their personalities upon the person.

There are the strong and dominant type unclean spirits, that enter a person and literally "raise hell" within the daily living pattern and behavior of a person. Often, these unclean spirits drive people crazy and possession is sought to take-over the person's body. Can an unclean spirit drive a person to commit murder or kill themselves? The answer is yes!

There is a very fine line of thought that guides each and every one of us. The unclean spirits can evoke their thoughts into our thought channels that would make an unaware person believe it was he/she that created the thought. It is this one point the author realized there is a great danger to mankind. Some of the people that have committed heinous acts against another person, could not understand why or how they did what they did.

Many persons in prisons and mental institutions are not sick, they are possessed. The voice that they thought was from God or from themselves was actually from unclean spirits within them. Most of these people didn't even have a chance to realize who or what really drove them to act. The absence of judicial mandate proves this.

There are very few books out on this subject. Someone had to write it and provide a meaningful source of "evil behavior." Someone had to write a book that will deliver one from this grasp of the devil.

The feeling of "being drained of energy" is an indication of the presence of unclean spirits. To explain this feeling, you can compare several souls directing one body to act. Awareness, control of one's self, and strong praying can force unclean spirits within you to retract to a position of docility.

To prove this point, the dirty thoughts that enter your mind can be removed or eliminated by rebuking the causation of such thought each and every time you have a dirty thought. By the second month, your thoughts should be much improved. You have to view the wrestling away of your own body and mind from unclean spirits as the "spiritual war."

The battle is not a physical battle but direct with an extremely well organized spirit world. There are princes and principalities to manage the spiritual warfare. Without real knowledge, you are just swinging at the wind—you cannot hurt those spirits which are seeking to kill you. With real knowledge of the spirit world and the scriptures, you can be the "tormentor."

When Jesus said in **Luke 10:17–19—I give you power over all the powers of the enemy, and nothing shall by any means hurt you.** This authority was given so that you could survive in your life, in this world of satanic evil. It was given to make you the "tormentor", instead of the tormented. Claim it and use it. It is your God given right.

Years ago, an elder from the Methodist church came to my office and despite his cheerfulness, he told me that he had cancer. I asked, did you pray to be cure? Yes, only if it is God's will. I asked him, who taught you to pray like that? Don't you want to be healed? Yes, but it's up to God. If I could do it, I surely would like to smack the head of the idiot who started this—"if it's God's will."

Mercy on the hundreds of thousands of professing Christians who died if it was God's will. Does God want to control your will? Far from it, He wants to get rid of the evil in you and that includes the evil that is killing you. I asked the elder to hold hands in pray with me and we prayed, "Lord, it is Your will that this brother is healed of cancer." He called me three days later saying that the doctors found no cancer in him, that he was healed. You have got to realize to take charge of your life and to exercise your God-given rights and powers. God gave us power over the powers of the enemy, so that you could have victory.

The greatest blockage to your victory is the satanic undermining of your rights, authority or the real truth that was given to you by Jesus. The truth will set you free. Find out what truths there are for you. You are the only person that can make the greatest change in you! If you do not end up with the Holy Spirit working inside you, then struggle with the scriptures by yourself and ask the Holy Spirit, who will teach you all things. A church that does not move you to a strong communion with the Holy Spirit is a very weak church and is not spiritual.

If you are a long time Christian reading this book, you should know what I am saying to you. If you are a new Christian or have not accepted Jesus as Lord, then read the Bible (preferably King James version) and the Apocryphal. Ask God the Father to send His Holy Spirit into you to teach and guide you. If you don't unleash the powers described in this book, it does you no good.

Yes, the unclean spirits will subject themselves to you by the name of Jesus, but what would it profit you? It's far better to have your name in the book of life and enter heaven.

Chapter XIII

Exorcism

The actual act of exorcism is the casting out of unclean spirits from a person; yet, it is this act that healing takes place. A more accurate description of exorcism is "scriptural healing", because it is the same act that Jesus used to heal He would command the unclean spirits to come out and then, the people were healed. If you read **Matthew 10:1—healed of all manner of sickness and disease.**

Scriptural healing is a more accurate terminology, but can you join me in a great revelation about this scriptural healing—almost anyone can do it! There are great ministers, whom God gave the gift of the Holy Spirit to heal. Many of these ministers do not believe you can heal others, saying you are not gifted with the Gift of Healing from the Holy Spirit, so you cannot heal others. Can you heal—yes, you can and very strongly. It is God's word doing the healing.

Some of the wonderful Christians that are around me have encountered experiences of "scriptural healing." Our missionary to the Philippines, knelt on his knees and deeply asked me to pray for him for the gift to cast out spirits. He did this moments after he witnessed his friend being knocked off her feet after I pointed my finger at her some 15 feet away. I commanded the unclean spirits within her to speak from her mouth and after they spoke, I cast them out. The next day, I departed Manila, and she wrote a very dear letter to me, that she went to the doctors the next day and they declared her healed. Both her and our missionary were spreading the word of God.

By the way, I did lay hands upon our missionary to cast out unclean spirits and the very next day, he cast the unclean spirits out of members of his family. I cautioned him to have an experienced minister around when he does this, but he said, he couldn't find anyone in the ministries or churches that could cast out the unclean spirits.

When you complete this book, you should be able to cast out unclean spirits by yourself. But, I do not recommend it, without an experienced exorcist/minister present. I did it by myself, but my personality can be described as "very feisty" and considerable understanding of all the relevant scriptures were taught to me and put to memory.

The world's greatest exorcists were my teachers, a tremendous amount of praying, and a very serious desire to search the scriptures had been undertaken. I didn't just read a book and begin the exorcism—and neither should you.

Power up in the Word, get with the Holy Spirit, get in prayer and fasting—then put on your helmet of salvation, gird thyself with the truth, your shield of faith, and the sword of the Spirit—then you can be ready to slug it out with the devils in your life. By doing it this way, you will win. When you see the impact of the Sword of the Spirit come from your mouth, light from your eyes, your fingers turning gold bright—you have arrived.

To be less than fully prepared can open you and your loved ones for satanic attack and battle. If they cannot get to you, they will break you down to your knees by destroying your loved ones. You have to pray for their protection and for their growth of communion with the Holy Spirit. If you have a regimented life of constant prayer and searching of the scriptures, you can make it. If you expect to be a weekend hero, it is the stupidest thing you could ever do.

After you enter this warfare, the satanic world will stop sending privates against you and will commence by sending generals, stealth bombers, and seal teams against you!

Unless you had a recent discussion with Jesus, it becomes very unclear as to which comes first—the authority of the Word or the Power of the Word. This is the foundation start point for "scriptural healing." Do you just use the Power of the Word or are you standing on Authority? Where does the power or the authority come from? Can you have power without authority? Yes.

Can you get authority and then exercise power? Yes. Well, how did some of the great ministers get their powers? Some from praying, fasting, standing on the word, and some just began to heal and cast out. Isn't it as the Spirit wills? Can you pinpoint it? Some ministers try for years to get certain gifts and cannot, why? Can you understand why it is important for you to obtain greater understanding of the spirit world before you commence your spiritual operations affecting the spirit world?

This is why it is necessary to understand this book in its entirety prior to your absolute destruction of the satanic kingdom—a good idea but don't do it all by yourself! It is clear for me to realize that two additional books are necessary to give real strength and power to the readers. Time permitting it will be done. These books should be out in 1999 and 2000.

To keep the initial book in fundamental context, the Exorcism Section is divided into the following segments:

A. Authority of the Word
B. Power of the Word
C. Angels
D. Scriptures for Exorcism
E. The Commands
F. Subject's Behavior
G. Expulsion
H. Subject's Reactions
I. The Important Follow-up—Keeping Unclean Spirits from Returning

FOREWORD: It takes real love to be a great exorcist or minister of the Lord. Most people find it most difficult to show love a stranger in need; yet, Jesus did. Even at the dying of the cross, with His bowels screaming out and the diminished blood levels causing extreme reactions to His body and eventually the heart failure—He said **"Father forgive them, they know not what they do."** This dying love will be known to those who pick up the cross.

It isn't easy to destroy the works of the devil, but that is exactly what you will be capable of doing—after you have comprehended the content of this book. When you commence, know you will be going into a battle. Do not seek this power for fame, for you will not be famous. Do not seek this power for wealth, for you will not be wealthy. Seek this power for **"working with the Lord" (Mark 16:20)** and He will work with you confirming His word with signs and wonders.

PRAYER OF PROTECTION: Prior to any exorcism or event which involves any spiritual encounters, it is always necessary to pray for protection. You are dealing with forces which you cannot see or touch, but they can see and enter you. The battle has been one-sided. In **Ephesians 6:12–18, for we wrestle not against flesh and blood, but against principalities, against powers, against the rulers of the darkness of this world, against spiritual wickedness in high places.**

Wherefore take unto you the whole armor of God, that ye may be able to withstand in the evil day, and having done all to stand. Stand therefore, having your loins girt about with truth, and having the breastplate of righteousness; and your feet shod with the preparation of peace; above all, taking the shield of faith, wherewith ye shall be able to quench all the fiery darts of the wicked. And take the helmet of salvation, and the sword of the Spirit, which is the word of God; Praying always with all prayer and supplication in the Spirit, and watching thereunto with all perseverance and supplication for all saints.

The battleground has been described, the enemy has been identified, the armor and weapon has been given—now the soldier prepares for the battle. As in the moments of battle in all lives, the warrior prays to God for strength to defeat the enemy and to return to his/her loved ones safely.

> **PRAY**: Prior to all exorcisms—that the Holy Spirit will cover you and your loved ones and those who are present and their loved ones. *That no unclean spirit will be able to enter into your bodies. That Holy Angels surround you and knock-out all unclean spirits, satanic spirits, and all manner of sicknesses and diseases. That they will never enter anyone again, in the Name of Jesus.*

A. AUTHORITY OF THE WORD: There is only one authority of the Word and it is God Himself. Jesus was the Word and the Word was God. What comes from God's mouth does not return to God empty. He made all creation with His Word and all creation is held by the power of His Word. His angels upholds His Word. When God gives you power, He gives you His angels. The angels have the task to execute His Word.

What we read in the scriptures, must be clearly understood in two categories—Holy Scriptures and Holy writings. The Holy Scriptures includes the Word spoken by God.

The impact of the Word is far reaching and is immutable. The Holy writings are those words in the bible written by men inspired of the Holy Spirit. When we read the New Testament and read in a "red letter" Bible the Word spoken by Jesus or the Father—the Word is holy and must be obeyed by all creation and all creatures. The Holy writings are testimonies, historical reference, and very helpful truths for our lives. The application of the Word in the bible must be understood in this manner.

It is God's authority that can move creation and the creatures within it. Our authority of the Word, is that which is given to us by God. There is nothing, that creation can receive, except that which is given by God. By who else other than God are we able to live or have existence? When God gives us His Word, we have power. When God gives us the power of His word, we have power. What is the difference? The often misunderstood phrase—power of the Kingdom of heaven means angels created by God to uphold His Kingdom of Heaven (Jesus).

The Kingdom of God means the government of Jesus. Thus, when Jesus gives us His angels to hold His Word, we have been given the power of His Word. Did Jesus give us this power? Yes. If He gave us this power, then we should have access to this power. Yes. Where is this power? How does it work? **Mark 16:17, 20—and these signs shall follow them that believe; In my name they shall cast out devils; they shall speak with new tongues; and they went forth, and preached everywhere, the Lord working with them, and confirming the word with signs and wonders.**

Most churches today do not teach or train the congregation as to this very important verse of the bible. The church itself has been "sterilized" from spirituality. The devil has removed from the church the most important power of man—the God created spiritual powers given to man. Very few churches are spiritual and fewer members are spiritual.

The authority of the Word is from God and is God working with you.

B. POWER OF THE WORD: God upholds His Word through His angels. All creation is held by the power of His Word. Throughout the bible there are many references to angels: answering prayers to God; ministering to the saints; carrying out God's commands; and hundreds of different functions.

The power of the Word is the angelic force sent to carry out the fulfillment of the word. In **Genesis 28:12,13—Jacob dreamed and saw a ladder reaching up to heaven; and he saw angels ascending and descending; at the top of the ladder was God.** The angels ascending the ladder are bringing prayers of the saints to God while the angels descending are bringing the answers from God to the saints. It is the descending angels that have the power of the Word.

The descending angels are bringing the answers to your prayers as did Gabriel in the book of Daniel. But Gabriel took weeks to get back to Daniel with his answer because the Prince of Persia fought against Gabriel. Gabriel had to get Michael to help him get through. Your angel brings the answer to your prayers. Your angel also will uphold the "power of the kingdom of heaven" for it is your angel's duty.

The following are scriptural excerpts on the power of the word:

Luke 10:19—Behold, I give unto you power to tread on serpents and scorpions, and over all the power of the enemy; and nothing shall by any means hurt you.

John 1:12—but as many as received Him to them gave He power to become the sons of God, even to them that believe on His name

Acts 1:8—But ye shall receive power, after that the Holy Spirit is come upon you.

Matthew 16:19—and I will give unto thee the keys of the kingdom of heaven; and whatsoever thou shalt bind on earth shall be bound in heaven; and whatsoever thou shalt loose on earth shall be loose in heaven. After the cross and the resurrection, Jesus said to His disciples, "**all power has been given to me on earth and heaven.**" When you combine this with **Mark 16:20** and Jesus will be performing signs and miracles, confirming His word?we bind or loose on earth and Jesus binds or loose in heaven.

Luke 9:1—then He called His twelve disciples together, and gave them power and authority over all devils and to cure diseases

Matt 10:1; Mark 6:9; Matt 8:16–17;

C. ANGELS: As Paul wrote to the Hebrews, **Hebrew 1:14—are they not all ministering spirits, sent forth to minister for them who shall be the heirs of salvation?** Angels are ministering spirits for those who are the heirs of salvation. Who are the heirs of salvation? Those who will go to heaven. Who will go to heaven? Those who are born of the Holy Spirit and of water baptism.(**John 3:5**) The Holy angels had been assigned to you to minister to you. The very definition of the word angel is messenger. They are the messengers between the corporeal and the spirit worlds.

Angels literally do perform the same types of functions like man, but with a greater and more defined purpose. There are people that do not know why or what they are to do in this world. In this life, I have been called a sluggard or bum by my lack of purpose. I need plenty of sleep and plenty of food. It suits me fine if I do nothing for days. Except, by my calling, there are many things that I do and become unrelenting. I know there is a real God and it really bothers me that He knows how lazy and fallible I really am.

Even the knowledge of this book has been acquired for many years, but it really was a Herculean feat to put it to print. The Holy angels can see God and know about an Almighty God, with an emerald bow around Him to symbolize His eternal nature and lightning and thunder flashing around Him. All those who are in or have entered the spiritual world know this and there is no misunderstanding that He is Creator. There is no doubt in my mind, that if everyone knew about God, they would be praying everyday. Before Jesus died, He said, they would not do what they did, if they knew who Jesus was.

For those who are to go to heaven, you have a guardian angel. Even Jesus was called an angel and His work gave us all a great message. The angels: protect; minister; bring your prayer to God; perform untiring tasks for you; bring you an answer from God; and will be judged by you for what they did or did not do. They have a soul, emotions, intellect, and a great interest in the role of faith in your life. For the sake of this book's purpose, we will be descriptive of the aggressive nature of angels.

One of the most amazing events of my Christian life was to witness the casting out of unclean spirits by a visiting pastor. In 15 minutes, the pastor just shouted at people from a local church, whom I knew well, the word "get out" and everyone (more than 300 people) was knocked-out and off their feet. He pointed his finger at people and they flew off their feet. Wow! What is this! How can anyone do such a spectacular thing? It was from this great moving of the Holy Spirit, that I became interested in exorcism.

The power of the pastor that evening were angels. The word "power" and "angels" are the same. It is an angel that knocks the unclean spirits out of people. It is an angel that carries out the "power" of the Word. The angels conduct the great spiritual warfare that exists all around us everyday. By angels (fallen angels), Satan sends them against us. It is also by angels we fight the spiritual warfare. In **Luke 10:17–19, Jesus gave us 'power' over all the 'powers' of the enemy and nothing shall hurt us**. God gave us angels to help fight for us.

Jesus said that if He wanted to He could call twelve legions of angels (**Matthew 26:53**), that one legion is 6,000 angels. In **Isaiah 37:36**, one angel killed 185,000 soldiers in one night. If you multiply, 72,000 angels times 185,000 you have 13,320,000,000. So Jesus could have at His disposal the "power" to kill everyone on the earth more than 10 times over. He knew that He could have conquered the Romans—so did the apostles.

You need to understand this point, for without this "power"/"angels" you cannot fight a spiritual warfare of evil spirits coming against you. The angels protect you from harm, **Job 1:10? hast not Thou made a hedge about him, and about his house, and about all that he hath on every side?** Even Satan's own confession that he could not get to **Job** because of this hedge around **Job**. What was this hedge? Shrubs? Angels. When I first discovered this point in **Job**, I prayed everyday for three weeks that God put a Holy Angel in my house, that I did not want any evil spirits to enter my home.

One day, our church elder came to our home and as she entered into our home she spun around screaming and nearly knocked me down trying to get out of the house. Then she sat down on our steps lighting up a cigarette in great nervousness. I asked her, "What had happened?" She said there is a great angel in your house. Then it dawned upon me, that God answered my prayer and sent a mighty angel to keep evil spirits from entering my home. From the way our church elder looked, she had unclean spirits in her and they got scared when they saw the angel. Try this for your home.

One of my pastor friends was going to his church one night, when someone accosted him with a knife and demanded his money or his life. He said, "You can't kill me, there is an angel holding your hand." The thug couldn't move his hand and got scared and dropped his knife and ran away. Why do you think they are called guardian angels? By this time, your church would call the nut house for you. What does the scripture really say about angels and power of the kingdom of heaven and of your belief?

It takes your step of faith to begin to believe. My first exorcism came after I saw the spectacular revival meetings that happened in churches, after I studied with the "Holy Spirit filled" ministers, and read hundreds of books about the Holy Spirit, angels, and satanic warfare.

One day a Catholic lady asked us to pray for her, because she had terminal cancer. We prayed with a group of pastors, but she was still ill. Finally after being told she would die in one week, she begged us to come to pray for her. I prayed before going to her home and upon arriving, she had lost a great deal of weight and was very pale. She could only drink half a glass of milk as her entire meal. She could barely stand upright. I was moved to take on the unclean spirit within her and shouted at the spirits inside her. She began to shake all over, her hands were trembling, and she was breathing in large heavy gasps. I knew the unclean spirits within her were going to come out. I touched her temple and she passed out. She was out like a light, so after 20 minutes we left. Later her sister and her husband called in great enthusiasm, she got up and asked to eat a T-bone steak! She lived for another one and half years, but had a reoccurrence after she went back to her Catholic church.

It is a great victory to knock them (unclean spirits) out of people. Over the years, many unclean spirits were exorcised. People were being knocked off their feet by: just pointing my finger at them; looking at them; shouting at the unclean spirits inside them; laying on of hands upon them; and praying for them. The angels were working with me as I was working with Jesus. He was confirming His word with signs and wonders. (**Mark 16**)

As mentioned earlier, the Pastor of the leper colony, was given a leprosy healing angel by God after he contracted leprosy himself, but unselfishly asked God to only preach to the lepers. God healed him and sent a great healing angel for leprosy that freed more than two thirds of the lepers. A statute of the leprosy angel is in the midst of a beautiful garden on the Island, stepping on a leprosy unclean spirit and killing it with a spear.

This is what has to happen, to free the people. This is what the warriors of God are given to fight against an unclean spirit that brings disease and sickness that kills. For those ministers who teach only salvation, great! But after salvation, move to a Holy Spirit filled church that teaches/preaches your spiritual growth and how the Word, the Holy Spirit, angels, your armor, can be effective against a structured satanic world.

You must be in a position to direct the angels in a spiritual warfare. You must be filled with the Holy Spirit. You must know the word of God. You learn to fight against a ruthless enemy that is trying to kill your family, your friends, and the loved ones around you. If you cannot fight the good fight, or you cannot become a "tormentor"—then give this book to someone who can. If you cannot fight the spiritual warfare, then raise up someone who can.

Angels are very powerful beings. Throughout the scriptures, whoever saw an angel became very scared. They not only look very powerful, but they are fiercely strong.

My friend Pastor Augustine Chiedozie, experienced death many years ago and went up into heaven. He saw this very bronze like angel about 10 feet tall. No one has ever seen an angel that looks like cupid, nor has anyone seen a female angel I am talking about angels and not unclean spirits. Some of the angels around great pastors are very large and powerful. They know why they are there and serve their directives of God's word very well.

For those who have angels around them and know what their callings are, but continue to sin against God—it is possible the angels, who have intellect and emotions, can also sin. If they commit a sin, they become a fallen guardian angel around these people. There are people whom we know that whatever they do, they cannot do what is right. These fallen angels must be removed from them, in order to survive. This might sound esoteric, but this could explain peculiar behavioral patterns and constant disastrous results.

When you are into the spiritual warfare, you have to be tough. For many of you, you have not experienced a "rough" childhood as I have and therefore you may have been fortunate enough to have lived a pleasant childhood, full of good deeds and quiet times. When you have knowledge and understand what is happening around you, how the satanic hierarchy is killing and tormenting everyone—don't get mad, get even.

In circumstances of real war, the most gentle of people have excelled in killing the enemy. Sergeant York was a bible living Christian who didn't want to kill. He resisted the draft, but was inducted and sent to the front lines. After he saw his fellow countrymen die, he excelled in killing and capturing the enemy. Most Christians would feel the same, had they experienced the same knowledge and understanding.

Your angels were created for such a warfare. Build a hedge of angels and work with them. There is a series of realizations prior to "working" with your angel(s). The scripture is very effective with all spiritual activities, including: warfare; working with angels; moving of the Holy Spirit, both within and without; the authority and power of the saint; how Jesus is continually working with the saints, by mediation, confirmation of the word, and the sending of the "power of the word", which is part of the "power of the Kingdom of Heaven" and the development of signs and wonders working with angelic beings in your lives.

It becomes all consistent and "deductive in knowledge" once a person really understands the spiritual definitions and framework of the spiritual world. For example, whenever we view the terminologies of the scripture with the "synonymous" spiritual meaning of the word or phase (*power means angels*) we can realize the spiritual meaning.

Here are some main principles that would assist you in the understanding of this very important point:

1. The holy scriptures, spoken by God or Jesus are irrefutable and must be put in reasonable context. The problem arises from our interpretations and failure to see the spiritual meaning of the word. For the holy scriptures, the spiritual meaning can and often portray an "allegory" to the literal meaning.

   The reading of scripture can be meaningful, even out of context, when the word is "sent" to a situation and not the situation drawing a conclusion to the "word." Most ministers would be very hesitant to expound in this "unorthodox" manner, but I am calling it as I have seen it. If you can grasp the framework which I am drawing for you, then you will be able to comprehend the spiritual world and work within it. Allegory as defined by Origen in 250 A.D., is to spiritualize the meaning of the scriptures, instead of taking their literal meaning.

2. The angels protect you and also fight for you. It is the case throughout the scriptures, both Old and New Testament. But Jesus gave us His authority and power from heaven to fight the good fight. Angels kill, capture, and bind as well as loose. **Luke 10:19—Behold, I give unto you power to tread on serpents and scorpions, and over all the power of the enemy: and nothing shall by any means hurt you.** Jesus gave you angels over all the angels of the enemy, and nothing shall hurt you. The full faith and understanding of this scripture gives you the "safest place on earth"—to receive angels from heaven having power over the angels of this world ruled by Satan.

The angels from heaven carry the "power of the Word" from God, which are answers to your prayers. The angels act upon the Word of God. The angels are directed by the Holy Spirit within you. The Word has Spirit and life, meaning the Holy Spirit. The angels uphold His Word. The angels can bind and loose unclean spirits from you.

3. In **Matthew 10:1—and when He had called unto Him His twelve disciples, He gave them power against unclean spirits, to cast them out, and to heal all manner of sickness and all manner of disease.** Jesus gave us angels against unclean spirits and to heal all manner of disease and sickness. The angels will fight against unclean spirits, to cast them out. You have the "authority" to have angels cast out unclean spirits from you and other people.

There was a reason why Jesus stated in **Mark 16—for these signs shall follow those who believe—they shall cast out unclean spirits...** One of the most dangerous weapons that Satan has devised is mankind against mankind. The intrusions by the spirits of unsaved people in our bodies and thought processes. To this main ingredient, add the lack of knowledge (**Hosea 4:6—My people are destroyed for lack of knowledge**), a non-spiritual knowledge or no knowledge—can only end in our destruction.

There is a high frequency of relatives who have died and found themselves in a spirit world ruled by the devil, panic sets in, then realization, then fear, then subjugation by evil spiritual forces within the satanic hierarchy. Who do the relatives "enter"? Who do they know best? Who would be the comfort zone for them? Who would the satanic forces desire them to enter? Why?

If this was a pure military operation, even the generals would pick targets for their forces that knew best "how to deal" with them, who would know them best. The answer to all these questions is their relatives. This is a real sad part of this spiritual warfare. The devil is not stupid, he would have you fight against your own and stand back and laugh at both. Can you exorcise your relative? Can your break their hold on you? Can you command them to enter into swines? Can you tell them to get out of your life? There is only one answer—you must exorcise whoever it is, from you, before they kill you.

Your angels know what to do and what must be done. Work with them and draw power and fire from heaven to give them the effective weapons to cast out all unclean spirits and all disease and sicknesses from you. The command must come from your mouth. By the usage of the Word of God—Jesus, by the usage of the Holy Scriptures, by the moving of the Holy Spirit within, you can defeat all the enemies, the satanic hierarchy, and the weaknesses of your mind.

One of the most beautiful sights and experiences is to command the unclean spirits out of someone very sick and see your angel knock them off their feet. The natural response is—wow! It is not a beauty contest, it is a real fight.

Set aside your mannerisms and see how some "heavenly brass knuckles" feel in your hand. Don't hit them with a slap, level them with a nuclear blast. I say this not in jest, but to allow you to realize what it is going to take to get an evil manifestation out, who was trying to kill one of your loved ones. Take it from me, having been in so many fights, the professionals usually take one strike to take out an opponent. When you have to hit an opponent many times, you are too weak against him and you will probably get in real trouble and most probable, your enemy will end up defeating you. You must learn to take out an enemy at the first opportunity and very quickly.

D. SCRIPTURES FOR EXORCISM: It is most appropriate for the readers to know the important scriptures, prior to getting into the processes of exorcism. Look at it as "loading your gun." It will strengthen you spiritually and you will experience the Holy Spirit operating with you.

A list of scriptures are:

1. *Authority*: **Mark 16:17–20; Matthew 10:1; Matthew 8:16–17; Mark 6;7; Luke 9:1,2; Luke 10:17–20; Matthew 16:19; Acts 1: 8; Acts 10: 38**

2. *Power:* **2 Peter 1: 3; 2 Timothy 3: 5; 2 Timothy 1: 7; John 14:12; John 14:14; Roman 4:17; John 1:12; Mark 16: 20; Luke 13:20; 1 Corinthians 2: 10–14, 16;**

3. *Commands:* **Matthew 16:1; John 14:14**

E. COMMANDS: This section bases the "usage of the Name of Jesus" as the authority, by which all knees shall bow. In exorcism, they are the most powerful words you can say. "Jesus" is your authority. The Name of Jesus is your authority. You can apply this most powerful weapon in the following manner:

The following commands are only for the exorcism of Christians. You "must never command" or exorcise any non-Christian, it is very dangerous. They are outside of God, then God does not protect them.

1. In the Name of Jesus, I command you—this means your command is **IN THE AUTHORITY OF THE NAME OF JESUS**

2. By the Name of Jesus, I command you.—this means your command is **BY THE AUTHORITY OF THE NAME OF JESUS**

Now the question is what is there to command? You are to keep in mind that you are confronting a satanic spirit that has been trying to kill, cause sickness, deceive the person that the unclean spirit is oppressing. There are no "slaps with wet noodles", you must destroy this unclean spirit from this person, otherwise, it will not depart.

What is worst is that if you are able to expel the unclean spirit(s) and the person from whom the unclean spirits are expel—does not understand how to keep them from coming back, then the unclean spirit(s) will come back with seven times more unclean spirits than before. **Luke 11:24–26—when the unclean spirit is gone out of a man, he walketh through dry places, seeking rest; and finding none, he saith, I will return unto my house whence I came out. And when he cometh, he findeth it swept and garnished. Then goeth he, and taketh to him seven other spirits more wicked than himself; and they enter in, and dwell there: and the last state of that man is worse than the first.**

The command is the God-given right/power/authority that God has given to you. There can be some variations, for instance, the people that copied the apostles, expelling unclean spirits from people (one can say it was "by the name of Jesus", while the apostles and those given the power by God, ("in the name of Jesus"). I have used both very effectively, as a Christian. *If you are not a Christian, I absolutely do not recommend the application of the knowledge of this book in any spiritual application.* You can get hurt by unclean spirits very badly, once they enter you, you will have a very difficult time to get them out or not at all. Should this happen to you, get to a Holy Spirit filled church and ask for help.

The command must be strong. Do not be polite or sympathetic, you are in a spiritual warfare and your opponent will try to kill you or your loved ones. In battles of all wars, men scream when they attack the enemies. Do you know why? They are faced with the ultimate challenge of survive or be killed. If you are a Christian and understand all the scriptures for exorcism, you cannot be killed. But you can be hurt and you can have unclean spirits enter into you. Remember God gives us power (angels) to protect and fight for and with us.

There is a very false doctrinal theology that some churches teach —"an unclean spirit cannot enter into a Christian." This is not true. The hospitals are full of Christians. Sickness/disease are brought on by unclean spirits. Those ministers who teach this false doctrine have no idea of the satanic world nor what an unclean spirit is. If such ministers preach or teach such false doctrines, they must make every effort to make it right for the congregation.

The command should be shouted firmly. Unclean spirits will test your resolve, your faith in the word, your belief in Jesus, and your position as a minister of fire. Some of you might reflect, well I have no right or power or authority, to expel unclean spirits from people. If you are like that, before you walk from what the author is saying to you, look at the loved ones around you that have suffered from diseases/sicknesses that have been caused by the unclean spirits inside of them. They are "tormented", because they don't know how to be freed and healed. The scriptures give you the weapons for spiritual warfare—use it!

The command should be directed at the unclean spirits within the person. Some of the very dear people, who had unclean spirits exorcised, looked like some of the nicest people you ever want to meet, but this is not exactly a social gathering, but a spiritual battle. Your spiritual knowledge of the authority of God has been given to help you against unclean spirits of torment. (Yes, I have been very guilty of swearing when I exorcise unclean spirits.) Instead of talking to the person, I make it very plain and clear, that I am only speaking to the unclean spirit within that person. Often, other church members are with me when I conduct exorcisms and they see me shouting at some very nice lady—"come out of her you @#!!" Obviously, it isn't what I teach ministers at the seminary, but you need to know this.

Most ministers are uneducated about the spirit world and they haven't spent enough time fasting and praying to receive the gifts of the Holy Spirit. Despite the criticisms that this book may create, it will bridge the void in the non-spiritual gaps for the laity and the ministers, who don't even know what an unclean spirit is or how to deal with them effectively.

The unclean spirits have emotions and despite a "hate-filled spirit world of Satan" they react very emotionally. For the more difficult unclean spirits, I use intensive intimidation to get them out. Sometimes it's like pulling teeth in the dentist's chair. There is tremendous pride, arrogance, anger, fear, hate, jealousy, and great sorrow. If you understand that the spirit world is of hate and these emotions above—versus a heavenly place of love, mercy, bliss, and justice—then you can see the battle lines. Spirits are frightened and do come apart emotionally and exit!

When you command, take command of the unclean spirits. This is a one way street, created by Jesus. Heads I win, tails you lose! When you stand on His word, there is no middle ground, no compromise, no surrender. If you do not exorcise in this manner—don't exorcise! When you first begin exorcism, be with an experienced exorcist. Don't do this as a home experiment. My dear pastor friend tried out exorcism by himself, and the skin on the person he was exorcising was melting and he tried everything in panic. When I first began exorcism in my home, a bunch of my pastor friends had the unclean spirit enter them and the whole room was screaming with pain in different parts of our bodies as the unclean spirit was attacking us.

Today, I allow church members to talk to the unclean spirits and shout at them until they come out. You have to know where you are going, what you want to accomplish, and be fully prepared for warfare. The unclean spirits should be "put down" at every opportunity. In one workshop on exorcism, someone asked, "How do you intimidate them?" "Easy", I explained, "I command you to drink all this toilet water and be flushed out with this toilet!"

One unclean spirit challenged me and said, "I bite her spinal cord like this" (making a biting gesture). I retorted, "I bind your mouth to be open and never to close again, in the Name of Jesus!" The unclean spirit said, "Oh, no!" The unclean spirits despise me so much, that they can see in my eyes, the mark of a "tormentor." Do you know how to torment an unclean spirit, now? The unclean spirits cannot stand this kind of treatment or aggressiveness. When the unclean spirit answered Jesus in **Matthew 8:29—what have we to do with you, Son of the Most High, have You come to torment us before our time?** The answer is yes!

The command must not be trafficking with unclean spirits as psychics/spiritualists/astroflighters want to do. Develop a short pattern of exorcising and commands for the unclean spirits. My main purpose is to exorcise them as quickly as I can. The following is the pattern that I follow from the numerous exorcisms:

1. **Who are you?** know their name

2. **How did you die?** tells what behavioral symptoms they bring and is their biggest weak point of emotions

3. **Are there other unclean spirits?** find out who they are

4. **What sickness did you or other unclean spirits bring in**? let you know what you are dealing with; command them to take the sickness out when they leave

5. **Who is the leader unclean spirit?** Have him/her speak to you, if you exorcise this leader spirit, then all the unclean spirits will leave; if there is a major disease, command the unclean spirit that is causing that disease to speak to you; when this unclean spirit is exorcised then that disease will disappear immediately—if the disease is still there, without any signs of rapid improvement, then the unclean spirit is still there. Another exorcism of that unclean spirit is needed. Normally, if you have their name, they must leave or commence a warfare of great torment against this unclean spirit—not only prayers for power, but constant commanding.

Recommendations: In warfare, for the gentlemen—be a tenacious warrior; for the ladies be the biggest intimidator you can be—but in all, don't let your resolve to expel be weakened or insulted by the unclean spirits.

"Never hit or strike any body." It is neither in scripture nor is it necessary. There are newspaper articles every year whereby someone church group beat to death someone they were exorcising! These people however well-meaning have no understanding or training on how to deal with spirits. They get to the stage where they talk to some nasty spirit causing some disease in one of their friends and they want to beat them and end up killing the person they are trying to save! It is the power of the Word of God in you that does the job.

F. SUBJECT'S BEHAVIOR: At the beginning, the first time exorcisms for the exorcist may be almost exasperating. For the first-timer exorcist, the unclean spirits may not react to any commands. Some of the famous exorcists have stood screaming at person for hours without any response. Until an aura of Holy angels surround you, the Holy Spirit shining from your eyes, your hands and fingers glowing like fiery gold—the unclean spirits in your subject may not react.

At some of the exorcism schools overseas, the beginning exorcists shot down the unclean spirits. To graduate from these schools, you must confirm the exorcism of two to three persons. Sometimes exorcists take hours to exorcise an unclean spirit. After you have gone through this time of trial for your resolve to exorcise unclean spirits, they will know who you are before you arrive. It is good training because you will know what it takes to get them out. Often, prayer groups take on an unclean spirit and prepare for a six-hour battle if necessary. Would you believe you can wear an unclean spirit down?

An experienced exorcist normally can command the unclean spirit to answer him within a minute. The very frightened unclean spirits or very stubborn ones take longer. For those types of stubborn unclean spirits, the author uses very strong methods of intimidation to flush them out into the opening. The very frightened unclean spirits will jump out suddenly. If they know you are rough, ruthless, or rotten—they want to get out quickly. So much for show!

Keep in mind, that this spiritual world has been undisturbed for thousands of years and they don't expect you to come along to challenge them in their own turf! When you can reach through to their world in power, the word gets around, they know who you are. Just like the exorcism attempt of the **Sceva sons** in **Acts**), the unclean spirits spoke to them and said, "Jesus I know and **Paul** I know, but who are you?" Let this book raise an army of warrior saints, deliverance ministers, exorcists, and spiritual fighters, who will take back what Satan has taken from mankind and our lives. *Show your love for the brethren and be a warrior saint.*

G. RESPONSE OF THE UNCLEAN SPIRITS: The techniques used by the author are many, but for the purpose of this book, "using the mouth of the person, to allow the unclean spirit to speak" will amaze you. Most people are "unbelievers", until they see and hear it themselves. You must fully prepare the person to be exorcised, by explaining what you are going to do. The actual using of the person's mouth is the greatest proof to those being exorcised—that there are unclean spirits within them. Once I asked a very gentle lady's husband to stand next to his wife, when I command the unclean spirit to speak, the unclean spirit within her used her mouth and said, "I am an emissary from Satan." He was shocked and bewildered.

You should educate the persons to be exorcised by reading the scriptures with them. Normally, I explain: what sickness is; where it comes from; what an unclean spirit is;

and my authority and the person's authority to expel them; and finally, how I will exorcise them.

There are three basic things which I ask each person before an exorcism:

1. I will only talk to the unclean spirit and not to the person. The person is instructed not to speak to me during the exorcism.

2. Just open your mouth very slightly and if the unclean spirit commences to speak, do not interfere, but listen only. The person is not to react on what is being said, because it is not that person who is speaking, but the unclean spirit within.

3. Do I have your permission to "get tough" with the unclean spirits? The person being exorcised must realize that I will torment the unclean spirits to get them out and use the authority given to me by Jesus. The person being exorcised must work together with the exorcist. Both must get tough with the unclean spirits.

Because there are numerous methods to exorcise unclean spirits the reactions by the unclean spirits have a wide variance. Unclean spirits have reacted by:

Screaming loudly; clinching the eyes of the person as tight as they could; falling down; being knocked-out and knocked down; being paralyzed; frantic breathing; shaking of the body; shaking of the hands; becoming stiff as a board; moving away from you in great fear; afraid of your touch; cannot look you in the eyes; does not want to hear; lying; boastful; and you name it, they can do it all.

When I take command over them in the Name of Jesus, they normally stand at attention and obey my commands; yet, all of the above have occurred. When there are many persons to be exorcised, then exorcisms go very rapidly. I normally cover some of the questions above, but expel them quickly. The knowledge of what unclean spirits by name, what diseases they brought in is important to those being exorcised, because most unclean spirits try to "re-enter" the same person after the exorcism. I have seen them expelled, then as soon as the person walks outside, they "re-enter" again. As discussed earlier, some exorcists immediately induce the Holy Spirit upon the person in the form of tongue speech, enabling the person to have the Holy Spirit in them.

To keep spirits from re-entry, you must explain clearly to the persons being exorcised that they must pray, on a daily basis and command any and all unclean spirits out of them and if they do not know who they are, then they must command "that unclean spirit" that is causing the sickness to get out at every chance they can. Having expelled many unclean spirits, I encourage sick people to smack the spot where they have sickness with their bible. The unclean spirits know clearly what the bible is and they are afraid of it. During some exorcisms, the unclean spirit is commanded to hold the bible as I am talking to them. They wince at holding the bible, but you can always tell if you are in command, order them to hold the bible, if they do not, you are not in command.

H. EXPULSION: The actual act of expulsion can be extremely subtle or a simulation of a Holyfield knock-out punch. Normally, the person being exorcised can tell that the unclean spirit has left or not. I have exorcised persons and they recant immediately that it was "like part of my brain was gone", "it's gone;" they sense their immediate healing; even good/bad behavioral traits gone; "something left me"—and all pain is gone!

The unclean spirit(s) within the person give indications of their willingness to leave—they indicate they will obey the Name of Jesus; they begin shaking all over, but especially at the hands; very heavy breathing; tremendous nervousness; showing great fear; how they obey you when you take command over them; they pass out or fall away from you; they cannot stand up; and a fear of the knowledge and Word of God that you possess (the more they fear you, the less likely they [the unclean spirits] will return to the person).

Subtle expulsion: When you command the unclean spirit to leave, they are defeated foes. They have lost. They realize they must leave; yet, many disobey the Name of Jesus, despite knowledge of their judgment by Jesus. When they leave, they enter a cold and hate-filled spirit world. They feel lost and fearful. One unclean spirit said to me, just before she left the person—"I'm sorry, Jesus." Most that leave subtly do not say anything, but leave. Because their departure is important, you must know whether they have left or not—the easiest way is to ask the unclean spirit, *why haven't you left?* If the unclean spirit answers, it is still in the person! If the person answers easily, then the unclean spirit has left.

Knock-out: The most apparent expulsion is the "knock-out" expulsion. I have seen even deacons of the church, knocked across the room. When I move my hands towards the person's forehead to touch them, they often crumple up or pass out before I actually touch them. Sometimes, I wave my hand at them and they fall over. The longest knock-out has been about 20 minutes with a lady who was in full spread of cancer over her body. The lady in Manila looked as if she had died, because her breathing was very slight, but she jumped up when commanded to do so. These knock-outs are dramatic and the results have been very dramatic. Despite being knocked-out, the unclean spirits seem to fall out of the person, like a ball just bounced out of them. For those persons who can see spiritually, you can see the unclean spirit in the person's face and body as well as outside of them. In either case, the unclean spirits show up as dark shadows in the person's face and a dark cloud like ball with a tail, outside of the person:

This is what the spirit of a person looks like outside of their body. A dark cloud that is transparent with tail on right side, normally touch the person's forehead in expulsions. When the unclean spirits know I am going to touch the person, they seem highly motivated to leave. On occasions, my fingers and hands are glowing a fiery golden light. My touch to their forehead is very quick, in which I grab the back of the head and the forehead with both hands. The exit points of unclean spirits are: eyes; ears; lower orbital nerves; nose; and the mouth. The entry points are: lower orbital nerves; nose; eyes; fingertips; and ears.

Exorcisms have been done by just screaming at the unclean spirits, using my thoughts and not my mouth, and they have left. There was a woman in a wheel chair, who I exorcised just by looking at her eye. That unclean spirit jumped into one of my church members standing nearby.

The actual expulsion can be dangerous, when everyone has not prayed for Holy angels to protect them from the unclean spirits. Even unclean spirits have jumped into me, during exorcisms, when I got angry. Then I normally excuse myself and go into another room and rebuke the unclean spirits immediately and strongly.

I. BUILD PROTECTION: After exorcisms, the persons being exorcised must agree to keep these unclean spirits from coming back. They are to incorporate a daily and regular pray time into their daily life. I was once asked, how to get an unclean spirit out of a person, who cannot seem to get it out. I asked what he was doing to get it out and he told me he was reading the bible everyday. I told him, since he understood the bible fairly well to stop reading the bible and just start commanding the unclean spirit to get out.

After exorcism, the person must understand and know clearly what his/her behavioral patterns are. That anytime they seem to be "out of character" they must rebuke in the Name of Jesus that new behavioral changes.

From my experiences, there seems to be an order of warfare:

—*Point of Dying:* If you resist the devil even to the point of dying and holding unto Jesus Christ as Lord and Savior, he will leave you; after this experience, you should dedicate part of your life to God

—*Holy Angels:* If you pray constantly for Holy angels to minister to you in great numbers and power, an aura surrounds you; your home is peaceful; there is much light(s) around you; the Holy angels attack unclean spirits and protects you from satanic angelic beings, as well as other persons

—*Effective Exorcists:* The exorcists seem to have a very strong command and knowledge of the scripture and how they are applied spiritually; they are not timid and have a heart to help the brethren; gifts of the Holy Spirit are operating in them, particularly discernment, healing, and faith; please keep in mind, these are only observed traits and not a prerequisite by any means; anyone can be an exorcist, but you must be totally prepared!

—*Discernment:* Prior to becoming an exorcist, one should pray and ask for the gift of spiritual discernment; the effectiveness of the exorcist is greatly enhanced by this gift.

—*Scriptural Understanding:* You must know the spiritual meaning of the bible; for the many believers stuck in apostate churches and taught the wrong doctrine—it is difficult and dangerous to become an exorcist; if your church does not have ministers or laity who can heal or exercise the gifts of the Holy Spirit, then it is highly probable that there cannot be any development of exorcists. My recommendation is to leave any church that does not add to your spiritual growth or receiving of the gifts of the Holy Spirit; if no one can see spiritually, then do not attempt exorcisms.

—*Prayer Group:* It is from many prayer groups that spiritual growth occurs; those who receive the gifts of the Holy Spirit can prepare themselves and others, to minister to others; often the most spiritual persons are those who pray for the gifts and for others; from the prayer groups the teaching of exorcism would seem the most likely support group.

—*Holy Spirit Church:* in every Holy Spirit filled church, all the gifts of the Holy Spirit are working; it seems like the most unstructured churches have the Holy Spirit operating; keep in mind that very few of the very large churches normally are able to develop the congregation's spiritual growth, but concern themselves towards programmatic ministries; there are few programs of churches that foster spiritual growth and development.

—*Daily Worship:* to remain healed and free of unclean spirits requires a regular regiment of worship, singing of hymns, spiritual growth, prayer, and constant expulsion of unclean spirits when out-of-character traits appear. An unclean spirit was asked how do you feel when this person sings to God, the unclean spirit contorted her face in grimace and anger; this same reaction surface when the unclean spirit was asked "how do you feel, when she prayers?" There is no doubt that all unclean spirits cannot stand a person praying and singing hymns all the time. The bible is greatly despised by all unclean spirits.

The easiest way to see if a person is demon possessed or not, is simply ask the person to read, **Rev 20:11–15—and I saw a great white throne, and Him that sat on it, from whose face the earth and heaven fled away; and there was found no place for them. And I saw the dead, small and great, stand before God; and the books were opened, which is the book of life: and the dead were judged out of those things which were written in the books, according to their works. And the sea gave up the dead which were in it; and death and hell delivered up the dead which were in them; and they were judged every man according to their works. And death and hell were cast into the Lake of Fire. This is the second death. And whosoever was not found written in the book of life was cast into the Lake of Fire.**

The last time I asked someone demon possessed to read this, he threw the bible away after reading it. You can believe it, that scripture, constant prayer, and worship has a good effect upon your life.

—*You, the Tormentor:* There is enough presented to you for a clear understanding to become a tormentor of unclean spirits. Jesus came to destroy the works of the devil, in **1 John 3:8?for this purpose the Son of God was manifested, that He might destroy the works of the devil.** You are in His will when you destroy the works of the devil.

Heal Thyself!

You can exorcise unclean spirits and sickness/ diseases from yourself by evoking direct commands. Self healing is when you become thse "tormentor" of the unclean spirits inside of you. Constant tormenting of the unclean spirits within you, worshipping to God, singing hymns will literally drive away the unclean spirits and the sickness/ disease they brought into you. Constant direct commands, *in the Name of Jesus*, will remove these unclean spirits. Add a little torment and mix it up and you will have your old self back again! It does work, you just have to do it!—*W.Yep*

Chapter XIV
Conclusion

It takes a lot of dedication to become a strong exorcist. The calling for the works of an exorcist is incessant. There are few laborers. The great rewards of seeing the oppressed freed cannot be matched in this world. When you see it, understand it, seek to grow in spiritual gifts—then you have joined the battle.

For those who professed to have already joined the battle, without a strong spiritual development of the gifts of the Holy Spirit working in you and a deep "spiritual understanding" of the scriptures, it will be difficult to fight. Many pray for those seriously ill and then they die. That battle was lost. Many of you profess it is God's will and cease to develop any spiritual gifts in a spiritual warfare, you will lose in your day of battle. Some of you will try your best, but "your best" was not good enough. Some of you profess wisdom and great understanding of the scriptures, but do not lay hands on the sick, because you cannot heal them, you have never joined the battle. Get it together.

Most Christians do not have any real understanding of spiritual knowledge; yet, all profess to be spiritual. **James 1:22—but be ye doers of the word and not hearers only, deceiving your own selves.** Less than 2% of the ministers have real understanding of this book. Less than 1% conduct exorcisms effectively. This book seeks to bridge the needed knowledge to understand, prepare, and battle in the spiritual warfare. The preparation is considerable, the lives saved are precious. When you deliver someone from spiritual oppression, then you know what kind of a great God you have and where you stand with Him.

The book was written as a "narrative" how-to book. The narratives were meant to add clarity to the scriptures used. The declared fallacies of the current churches were meant to awaken your understanding, those who seek God in their lives, and those needing the spiritual deliverance from this satanic intrusion. It is a sad commentary to view the Christian world with such a critical eye. The weaknesses must be raised, the solutions found, the correction placed, and the brethren served with a heart of tender mercy. If we, who are empowered to help the brethren and do not, our works will be burnt as stubble. You have heard the phrase, "for evil to have victory over us, it only takes good men to do nothing!"

There are many other methodologies and application of scriptures in exorcism, the scriptures covered in this book provide a basic foundation for understanding and application. There is great power in the scriptures contained in this book. Their proper usage was a great concern of the author. Because of the absence in the churches and seminaries to teach scriptural healing, it is given to you as a weapon of spiritual warfare for your lives. With any weapon, application is critical. When you achieve your first deliverance and see the great healing upon the faces of those who were held captive—then you can understand the author's hope for an emergence of a new type of Christian? the God empowered warrior saint!

When you first hear the voice of an unclean spirit coming on its own strength from the mouths of persons under their persecution, then you can understand the author's decision to teach the God given power, for it takes greater power to defeat the powers of oppression in this world. You can appreciate the God given power to us, when unclean spirits are subject to us through His Name.

Scriptural healing is needed in every church, seminary, denomination, and prayer group. The ministers do not often participate, since they have already achieved the minimum standards of prayer. Whether this knowledge is present within their repertoire of abilities, they need this knowledge to look over the sheep, so that "no harm" will come upon the members of the church. The shepherd's staff is hooked to be both a guide and a weapon for the sheep, so is the Word of God.

For those who may be offended by the brash nature and narratives of this book, my sincere apologies. To those who can look past my idiosyncrasies and flaws of character, to seek the truth and seek real spiritual growth, you would have met the goals of this book. May you be blessed of the Lord in your good works, who will work with you, confirming His Word with great signs and wonders.

See you in the **Sequel!** —*Demons Are Not Forever*!

Appendices:

Index

Biblical References

One-Sided View of Christianity

Working Definitions

Other Books By Wallen Yep

Index

2 Esdras (Unclean Spirit) 23, 65, 118

A
administrators 2, 62
allegory 88
angelic 21, 59, 118
angels 23, 62, 88, 117
animal 39, 58
Apocryphal 36, 75
atheists 60
authority 22, 74, 118

B
behavior 29, 72
bible study 35
Biblical references 113
books xii, 30, 74
Buddhist 40, 66
build protection 1
bum 83

C
casting out, cast out 6, 45, 120
Catholic 23, 85
cemeteries 72
Chiedozie, Augustine 86
child-like 73
Christianity vi, 10, 64
churches 1, 33, 65, 91
commands xi, 48, 81
confirmation 87

congregation 2, 39, 91
consensus theology 9, 10

D
death 7, 22, 64, 94
deliverance 3, 50, 95
demons vii, 19, 32, 105
discernment 7, 36
disease 1, 33, 82
doctors 28, 40, 77
doctrinal overview 5

E
economic 62, 120
energy 74
evil ix, 19, 46, 89
exorcism 100, 118
exorcist 6, 27, 67, 93
expulsion 97, 118

F
faith 1, 28, 49, 99
fingers 78, 98
foundation 78, 104
fundamentalism 60

G
Gabriel 32, 82
Gedara, Maniac of 24, 65, 70
gee-shun 118
Genesis 82

109

get even 33, 68, 87
Gifts of the Holy Spirit 3, 40, 92
good vii, 28, 60, 101
government 63, 81, 119
growth xiv, 30, 60, 100
guardian angels 34, 85

H
hatred 25, 59, 129
hedge 35, 84
Holy Scriptures 87, 119
Holy Spirit xi, 40, 97, 118
Holy Writings 81, 118
homosexuality 71
hospital 1, 40

J
Jacob's ladder 32, 119
Jesus 117, 119
Job 129
Judgment 20, 69, 119
judicial 70

K
kill 24, 47, 73
King, Jr., Martin Luther 31, 37
King James 23, 75
kingdom of God 81, 119
Kingdom of Heaven 81, 119
knock-out 72, 97

L
laity 2, 33, 65, 100
laying of hands 39, 121
leper colony 31, 48, 85
love vii, 35, 92, 129
lust x, 25, 67, 118

M
Matthew 27, 44, 77, 90
Methodist 75
methodologies xi, 6, 29
ministers xiv, 28, 50, 92
mystery spirit 11, 64

O
old testament 28, 39, 62
one-sided view of Christianity 115
oppression v, 20, 103, 120
out of character 24, 99

P
pandora's box xiii
part-man, part-animal 55
pastors, great 2, 24, 64, 85
personalities, split/multiple 58, 70
Philippines 51, 77
pick up the cross 17, 79
possession 20, 70, 120
power 119
power of the Word 119
prayer vii, 31, 83
prayer of protection xii, 79
principality 55, 120
protection xii, 78, 99
psychiatry 71
psychics 25, 60, 93
psychology 29, 71

R
religion 7, 25, 64, 122
rulers of darkness 18, 58, 120

S
Satan 19, 53, 92, 121

satanic hierarchy 22, 53, 121
science 9, 30, 66, 126
scorpions 45, 82, 88
scriptures x, 28. 64, 103, 117
scriptural healing 6, 45, 104, 121
secular xiv, 1, 54, 118
Sequel, The 118
serpents 45, 61, 82
Sheol 22, 65, 119
sickness 1, 28, 61, 97
spiritual battle xi, 34, 92, 120
spiritual warfare 9, 60, 103, 121
split personalities 66
statement of faith 1, 11, 122
subject's reactions 81
sword of the spirit xv, 17, 48, 78, 120

T
t-bone steak 85
therapy 71
thesis xiii, 71
thug 85
time ix, 26, 52, 91, 125
tormented v, 23, 68, 122
tormentor v, 32, 68, 122
tv evangelist 3, 19
two-edged sword 19

UV
unclean Spirits v, 18, 39, 64, 97
voice 74, 104

W
weekend hero 78
wicked spirit 122
witness 54, 83
Word, the xiv, 19
working definitions xii, 117

Y
Yee, Watchman 8
York, Sergeant iii, 87

Biblical References
(Used in This Book et. al. by W. Yep)

Scripture:	Purpose:
Acts 1:8	authority
Acts 10:38	method
Acts 19:12-17	authority
1 Cor 2:10-14, 16	discernment
2 Cor 5:8	appointment
2 Esdras 7:69-103	appointment
2 Esdras 7:79-87	discernment
Ephesians 6:12; 12-18	warfare
Genesis 28:12,13	angelic
Genesis 3, 15	enmity
Genesis 6:3	time
Hebrews 11:1	faith
Hebrews 1:14; 13-14	angelic
Hosea 4:6	life
Isaiah 37:36	angelic
1 John 3:8	authority
James 1:22	authority
Job 1:10, 12	angelic
John 14:14, 12	power
John 17	authority
John 1:12	authority
John 3:5	Holy Spirit
Joshua 1:5-9	power
Luke 10:17-19	authority
Luke 11:24-26	unclean spirit
Luke 13:11-17, 20	Satan
Luke 8:2; 9:1-2	authority
Mark 16	authority
Mark 16:16-17, 15-18	power, authority
Mark 16:20	confirmation
Mark 6:7; 6:13	exorcism, authority
Matthew 10:1	authority
Matthew 16:19	authority, power
Matthew 26:53	protection
Matthew 8: 16; 17	healing, exorcism
Matthew 8:29	time
2 Peter 1:3	authority
Rev 20:11-15	judgment
Romans 4:17	creation
2 Timmothy 1:7	power
2 Timmothy 3:5	warning

One-Sided View of Christianity

Spiritual World		Secular & Spiritual Worlds		
Cause	Effect	Christian Actions	Grace	Source
Devil	Liar, thief, Murderer, Accuser	Prayer & Fasting; bible, oil, laying of hands	Angel, Word, & Holy Spirit Gifts	GOD, Holy Spirit & Jesus
Angels	wars			
Ruler	economic			
Evil Spirit	religions			
Unclean Spirit	sickness oppression			
Frog	Lust			

Solution: "...To build a Scriptural Wall!"

Contemporary Christianity—	Seek the love of Jesus; pray; go to church; help others; witness; fast; obey the Word; read bible; build church; does not use spiritual Grace to defeat spiritual attacks.
What is wrong with this?	Contemporary Christian actions are ineffective against cause and effect; does not deal with the purpose of Jesus: **1 John 3:8.**
Problem:	We have failed the Great commission, **Mark 16:15-20;** we have no weapons of spiritual warfare; we are impacted everyday by spiritual effects; church has failed to be a deterrent against spiritual attacks; most ministers are not spiritual and do not teach or preach spiritual growth; seminaries have failed, they have taken conservative non-spiritual growth of spirituality In their denominations; there is no leadership; there is little deliverance.
The Solution:	*Christians must fully embrace God's grace—angels, Holy Spirit; and Word to achieve spiritual weapons that will be effective; the working of the Holy Spirit with the Word will become the Sword of The Spirit; angels will battle not only spiritual effects but the root causation; **John 17:17-18** we need to be sanctified by the word; be doers of the Word; walk in the Holy Spirit; know authority, power, and exercise power of the Word.*
Method:	Build a scriptural wall and use the Sword of the Spirit from you; know and claim your God given authority and power over all the powers of the enemies; grow in the gifts of the Holy Spirit.

IV. Working Definitions

The following is provided as a "working definition" for terminologies used in this book—as well as several others by the same author. As with definitions, the meaning of words have a tendency to change with time. In scriptural revelations, the moment of revelation will alter the way we use and define words. There is no comprehensive allegory of the entire scriptures, nor is it possible to compile at this time.

The great importance of categorizing and sharing revelations is not universal. Considerable obstacles remain within the agendas of men, denominations, churches, and seminaries. These obstacles do not benefit mankind as a whole, but serve to keep mankind in darkness. As revelation enters your life, add your spiritual definition to these meanings.

Allegory—To interpret the scriptures in a spiritual meaning instead of the literal meaning. Earliest of allegories used by Aristobulus, 2 BC pre-supposed that Moses taught scriptures using a Platonic philosophical meaning. While there are many allegorists who associated the "hidden meaning" of the words with philosophy, it was Origen in 250 AD that associated the scriptures with a spiritual meaning.

Authority—The rightful and true usage of the Word of God; the authority of the Word is from God and is God; to whom God gave His grace for the Word to continue to be filled throughout creation is the authority of the Word; the Holy Spirit gives His gifts to whomever He chooses. For those persons who have received His gifts, they have been given the authority of His gifts, then they can exercise the authority of God.

Command—A directive to spirits evoking the interactions of Holy Angels and the Holy Spirit. Effective commands utilize the "power of the Word" which is the strong presence of the Holy Spirit and fulfilling of the Word by angels. Unclean spirits are to obey such commands for they will be judged by Jesus for what they did or did not do.

Consensus Theology—The mainstream acceptance of doctrinal interpretations by the denomination, seminaries, ministers, and the laity. Contemporary consensus theology is non-spiritual, but highly literal and secular. Used as a determinant of the will of the congregation.

Deliverance—The expulsion of unclean spirits and spirit creatures from the body. Associated with this expulsion is the departure of the sicknesses brought in by these spirits. Deliverance is viewed as healing. This terminology is not used with the removal of satanic hindrances brought on by angelic beings; yet, it is appropriate to categorize this definition this way.

Discernment—A gift of the Holy Spirit that allows one to see spiritually. To spiritually see things. For the devoted of God, the gift may be "constant discernment." To be revealed by the Holy Spirit, the spiritual nature of something.

2 Esdras 7—The only place in Holy writings that tells what happens to the soul of an unsaved person after he/she dies. In Apocrypha of the Catholic bible, St. Jerome Version, 4th edition. These scriptures have been confirmed by exorcisms.

Exorcism—The act of casting out the unclean spirits and demonic spirits from a person; yet, this act is also an act of healing. A sign that will follow a believer, **Mark 16**. The confirmation of the Word of God by Jesus.

Fallen Angels—Angels that followed Lucifer from heaven. These angelic beings are the rulers of the satanic hierarchy and princes of principalities. They are very strong and their appearance is formidable. They cannot incarnate into man.

Frog Creature—A creature that enters a person upon the moment of sin in the person. These creatures cause lust and sensual turmoil in a person. Very little is known about them and their purposes.

Gee-Shun—Asian name for creature of the nervous system. An unclean spirit and demonic spirit will travel along the nervous system of a person. In **Sequel**, there will be a discussion of the activities of the unclean spirit in the nervous system.

Holy Scriptures—Those Words said by God in the scriptures. Often shown in red ink letter bibles. These Words are irrefutable and have strong spiritual meanings. Those Words said by God to the prophets, that were written down in the bible.

Holy Writing—Those words said by Holy Spirit inspired men. They include testimonies, instructions, and historical reference. There are limited spiritual meanings in these words.

Jacob's Ladder—In **Gen 28:12** the dream of Jacob who saw angels ascending and descending on a ladder that goes up into heaven. God was at the top of the ladder. The ascending angels bring up to God the prayers of the saints and God answers these prayers and give the power of God to the descending angels to come back and fulfill the prayer. God as Creator creates the answers to your prayers.

Kingdom of God—A government by God, in which God is king of kings, Lord of Lords. A heavenly government ruled in heaven. The history of Israel was a shadow of the Kingdom of God to come.

Kingdom of Heaven—Often used to be the Kingdom of Jesus, for example, the Kingdom of Heaven as come upon you, indicative of a present tense. Jesus working with you. The body of Christ of all who are saved. The usage and shift of the tense of the words from present tense to future tense still define the terminology with accuracy. Means Jesus.

One Hundred Twenty Year Rule—In **Gen 6:3** the time allotted for mankind by God for His Spirit to be with a person's soul/spirit. The time determinant for unsaved persons who died, for them to remain on earth. Upon 120 years, their souls go to Sheol, which is found in the center of the earth—the place for unsaved souls to await their judgment by Jesus in the Great White Throne Judgment. If an unsaved person died at the age of 40 years old, then their spirit roams the earth for the remaining 80 years.

One Sided View of Christianity—The contemporary non-spiritual understanding of Christianity by the majority of Christians. This condition arises from the non-spiritual teaching, preaching, and administration of churches. In this state, the

Christians cannot fight a spiritual battle. The weapons of spiritual warfare have been kept from Christians by those who administer the churches.

Oppression—The oppressing of another person's thoughts and personality into a person through the activities of an unclean spirit. Often oppression leads to sickness and infirmities. This act of oppression is a satanic directive to unclean spirits. Oppression can lead to possession, if the will of a person is so distraught that the person regresses until they "give up." At this point, possession takes place by the unclean spirit.

Possession—The taking over of a person's body by the unclean spirit (demonic possession) within. There are many people who are suicidal, even many Christians, who are unable to continue to respond to the world. At the point of possession, the unclean spirits take over. When asked who they are, they answer you in another person's name. Possession allows the unclean spirit to "live again"—the ultimate purpose of an unclean spirit.

Power—Means angels, both satanic and holy. The creation is upheld by the power of His Word. Holy angels uphold creation and the Word of God. Satanic angels are seeking to destroy the Word of God in mankind, but through the hierarchy, Holy Angels answer prayers and bring the creation of God to the saints.

Power of the Word—The Word of God made full by the interaction of Holy angels fulfilling His Word. Often associated with the Sword of the Spirit, but is not correctly defined as such. Can be an angel fulfilling the Word or God sending the Holy angels to fulfill the Word.

Principality—An area controlled by a fallen angel ruler or power. Principalities could be similar to countries or groups of countries or areas. The ruling angel maybe called a prince or ruler or power of the area. The macro type activities of princes—such as wars, economics, and religions.

Rulers of Darkness—Fallen angelic influences upon people to cover, hide, and discourage the revelation of the Word to mankind. The means are vague and unknown; lethargy and fear appears to be couple of the tools used by these rulers. There are many reasons why mankind has not come to the truth of the

Word of God. These rulers have orchestrated whatever means to keep mankind from knowing God.

Satanic Hierarchy—A fully structured system of angelic beings and the spirits of unsaved people and creatures that fostered the will of its ruler—Satan. Lies, deception, murder, stealing, accusations, sickness, dementia, and many other evils are the order of the day. Although there is a parallelism between this hierarchy and God's kingdom, the closer analysis of their hierarchy is very formidable and the means to stop its carnage upon mankind is to evoke the spiritual weapons which Jesus has authorized and to delegate to those who believe upon Him.

Scriptural Healing—Using the Word of God with interactions of the angels and the Holy Spirit to cast out all unclean spirits upon which all sickness and all diseases will depart a person. This is not the gift of healing from the Holy Spirit, but God's law to all creation, that all creation shall bow at the Name of Jesus, the Son of God. All spirits are to obey and those who disobey will be judged by Jesus for punishment. The stronger the scriptural understanding, with spiritual meaning of the Word, the longer the ability to cast out the unclean spirits, who brought the sickness into a person. This is exactly the way Jesus healed the people.

Sheol—The hollow place underneath the earth for the unsaved souls/spirits to await judgment by God. The souls and spirits of the unsaved will come to this place at the end of 120 years of existence of their souls.

Sickness—The physical illness caused from the dysfunction of the human body's normal processes. Dysfunction is the result of unclean spirits, who either caused such dysfunction or the introduction of such into a person's body. After the departure of an unclean spirit from someone, the sickness leaves and the person recovers. Scriptures, the laying of hands, pouring out of oil, the gift of healing of the Holy Spirit, the brazen serpent, and the priest having been the healing agents of God. As God said, He is the God that healeth you. These are His means. The Apocrypha states that doctors are to be consulted for sicknesses.

Spiritual Warfare—The usage of spiritual means to fight the satanic hierarchy's intrusion into your life. The angels, Word of God, the Holy Spirit are the best spiritual means for Christians to fight this hierarchy. Without these means there is no spiritual warfare but satanic carnage.

Statement of Faith—The principle that describes the faith and belief of a denomination. The limitations of that denomination in its understanding of the scriptures. This is neither scriptural nor an actual description of the body of Christ, which is to be composed of believers. The Statement of Faith has separated the believers and has caused the dispersion of religions, the author believes it was necessary in the past, but appears to be detrimental in the growth of occult religions.

Sword of the Spirit—The evoked power of the Holy Spirit in the Word of God. The Holy scriptures always contain the Word of God. It shall never return empty or unfulfilled. When angels uphold His Word and deliver the Holy Spirit in the Word—it will even divide the soul and the spirit of a person. The Word of God empowered by the Holy Spirit can separate an unclean spirit from one's soul.

Tormentor—The one who understands the satanic hierarchy and understands the spiritual weapons of the scriptures, who then proceeds to "torment" the unclean spirits out of the people's lives, by spirits, through the Name of Jesus. Until this occurs, people have been tormented by unclean spirits for thousands of years. The tormented people who exercise this knowledge will become the "tormentor" and the unclean spirits will become the "tormented."

Unclean Spirit—The spirit of an unsaved person who has died. Because the unsaved person's spirit has not been made "clean" by the atonement of the blood of Jesus on the cross, their spirits remains unclean. There is no repentance for those who have died and have not accepted Jesus.

Wicked Spirit in High Places—The angelic beings that cause perversion of God through religion, occults, and Satan worship. These perversions distort and tempt mankind into fallible and unholy perceptions of God. The religions and Satan worship around the world attest to mankind's perverted worship of other gods—to turn mankind not only away from God but also against God.

ially, that is **V. Other Books by Wallen Yep**

Available Now:

The Sequel

Demons Are Not Forever!

An in-depth treatise of the spirit world, unclean spirits, their functions, and their intrusions into our lives. The companion book to ***Who Are You?*** that builds upon the methods of exorcism and how to continue to get rid of your demons.

Unlike any book, ***The Sequel*** will enable and empower the readers to understand the spirit forces that cross over into the physical world. They can see us, but we cannot see them. It is time for you to understand that which exists all around us. Learn where and why sickness comes into our lives. It is time to take back your lives. Learn how to remove sickness from your lives.

Sequel accomplishes what the churches and ministers should have taught us—how to apply the spiritual weapons in a spiritual warfare and to have victory over demonic forces. See what an unclean spirit looks like outside of the body. A never before step-by-step description of very powerful spiritual healing with detailed narration. Understand the way to keep demons out of your body.

Our greatest dreams and plans for our lives have been the targets of spiritual intrusion. Upon comprehension of the book, your spiritual understanding would exceed the spiritual knowledge of most ministers. You will have the weapons for victory in a spiritual warfare. The sword is placed into your hands, the life before you can now be molded by you.

Order No.: ISBN 1-893534-03-0

Available Now:

Man Before Adam

A Correction To Doctrinal Theology

A cutting edge book that will provoke your understanding of the origin of mankind. Both science and the bible were correct, what remained in error was the interpretation of famous men who erred.

The compelling arguments mounts against contemporary doctrines—man came from a monkey between 4.2 to 4.7 million years ago or God created man in 4,004 B.C. In the search for evidence the stunning finding came—the missing link of mankind was found! Both evolutionists and creationists were wrong, the evidentiary findings have to be redefined. A more plausible interpretation must be made and erred doctrines of the past must be corrected.

With the use of Mitochondrial DNA trace back, the errors of interpretation becomes confirmed. We came from a race of humans before the creation of Adam and Eve. The bible, expositors, and scholars misinterpreted the bible. The time for the enormous truth has come.

Wallen Yep, author, educator, and consultant wrote one of the strongest "change agent" books for the 21st Century. Listed in *Who's Who in the World, Who's Who in America,* and more than 20 biographical publications. So pervasive a book, it becomes a must read for every church member, minister, scientist, teacher, student. We cannot have educated men make a monkey out of us. Christians cannot ignore the overwhelming scientific findings that man existed on earth well before 4,000 BC.

Man Before Adam (Order No.) ISBN 1-893534-01-4.

Early 2001 Release

How to Live Forever

The Secret to Life Without End

It was staring at mankind all along, but we possessed not the intellect nor the knowledge to grasp life. Once grasped all the secrets become so simple and plain that the continuum of life can be everlasting. There is a roadmap that exists, we still need to embrace it for our lives.

Knowledge comes to mankind by learning and by revelation. It took God to explain it, but mankind could not understand what He was saying nor why God did what He did. The key is not a microcosm of knowledge but the comprehensive view of life itself. The readers will enjoy the perceptions that structure our lives and our environment. The main ingredient to "live forever" comes from mankind itself, no one owns their life forever—we were created to live forever but failed our Crea-tor.

The scope of knowledge has been maligned. What we see today is a by-product of its fruits. We have been led like sheep into an abyss of destruction, not realizing that the destruction is to be upon ourselves. It's time to awaken and to see where we are headed and to search that which can remove us from certain doom. There is an avenue of escape, it was always there for us, but we could not distance ourselves from those who have no real knowledge—but only know how to eat, drink and be merry. Stop and find the right road to life. Wake up and live!

Order No.: ISBN 1-893534-04-9

Early 2001 Release Date

When Petals Fall

The Self Introspection of Sickness and Suffering

The author's views of human bondage of sickness and suffering. These include: A descriptive assessment of the elements of sickness, pain, and suffering. The separations of emotions from physical pain. The cage of helplessness and sickness. The reduced conclusion to seek deliverance. The God-given power of deliverance and the root causation of the sickness.

Many have known the negative aspects of sickness and the very great search for relief of the symptoms. Almost all strive for restoration as few seek deliverance from root causes. It becomes incumbent upon mankind to search and to know the physical and spiritual well being that exists.

A special account of the dying processes of the body when one becomes "a petal ready to fall." The cessation of body functions at death. As petals fall [wilt, or die], they are moved by the winds and the water in the environment they fall into. With life, our environment also changes, but there is still continuance. It is important to realize this continuance and where it will lead us. Before we fall from this life, we have choices.

It is an inescapable event of our living to reach this point of your fall as a petal. We must strongly prepare for this event to achieve a continuance that will be forever. The author shares the solemn experience of dying and its profound implications to our lives. The cross over to a spirit world is instant and is the most important event of our lives. Have you prepared for the "fall" of your petals?

Order No.: ISBN 1-893534-05-7

Summer 2001 Release Date

The Serpent Kingdom

The Rule of the Serpent

An intellectual probe into the time that was and the probable scenario of the most powerful physical world that ever existed. A journey into time before mankind as we know it. A description of his influence in the world that we live.

Did you ever wonder why there were dinosaurs? Why they became extinct hundreds of millions of years ago? If you had the appearance of an Iguanadon described in **Job 41** and ruled the world, what would your subjects look like? Would they have the image of people or would they have the serpent image that the ruler of the world possessed?

A fictionalized story elaborating upon the author's conjecture of what existed before mankind. A description of the ruler of this world and the undeniable traits that were inherent to the serpent kingdom. The immense hatred of a serpent against mankind made in the image of the God he serves. The Serpent's hierarchy which had to change due to the devices and cunning wisdom that it was created with. The dissent which consummated in the form of pride, power, hatred, predator relationships, and the absence of love.

Was it ever a wonder that a merciful and loving God raised His wrath and destroyed a world hell bent on destroying itself. From a world of predatory survival, rule of power, pride, lust-could mankind escape the inevitable conclusion—extinction?

Order No.: ISBN 1-893534-07-3

How to Order Books

Emerald Bow Ministries is please to provide the cutting edge books that can contribute to your spiritual growth and understanding. Also through this ministry are: books by Wallen Yep; Swords of the Spirit teaching tapes; forum discussions; and group training programs.

In the event that your local bookstore is unable to provide you with the copies below, please feel free to contact the publisher directly by either call or send to the mailing address below:

Call 1-800-780-3337 or Emerald Bow, 1945 N. Carson Street, Carson City, Nevada 89701. Please inquire about church or educational discounts for quantities of 10 or more books in a single order.

[ ] **Man Before Adam** —$12.95 ISBN 1-893534-01-4
    A Correction To Doctrinal Theology
[ ] **Who Are You** —$14.95 ISBN 1-893534-02-2
    How To Get Rid Of The Demons In Your Life
[ ] **The Sequel** —$14.95 ISBN 1-893534-03-0
    Demons Are Not Forever
[ ] **How To Live Forever** —$12.95 ISBN 1-893534-04-9
    The Secret To Life Without End
[ ] **When Petals Fall** —$12.95 ISBN 1-893534-05-7
    The Self Introspection of Sickness and Suffering
[ ] **The Serpent Kingdom** —$12.95 ISBN 1-893534-07-3
    The Rule Of The Serpent

Emerald Bow

1945 N. Carson Street, Suite 675
Carson City, Nevada 89701

Emerald Bow

About the Author

Wallen Yep, author, educator, and consultant wrote one of the strongest "change agent" books for the 21st Century. Listed in *Who's Who in the World, Who's Who in America*, and more than 20 biographical publications. So pervasive a book, it becomes a must read for every church member, minister, scientist, teacher, student.

www.ingramcontent.com/pod-product-compliance
Lightning Source LLC
LaVergne TN
LVHW011423080426
835512LV00005B/224